Early Years

Ralph Kirkpatrick

Early Years

With an epilogue by
Frederick Hammond

PETER LANG
New York · Berne · Frankfurt am Main

Library of Congress Cataloging in Publication Data

Kirkpatrick, Ralph.
Early Years.

1. Kirkpatrick, Ralph. 2. Harpsichordists – United
States – Biography. I. Title.
ML417.K66A3   1985   786.1'092'4 [B]   85-18029
ISBN 0-8204-0282-6

CIP-Kurztitelaufnahme der Deutschen Bibliothek

Kirkpatrick, Ralph:
Early Years / Ralph Kirkpatrick. With an
Epilogue by Frederick Hammond. – New York;
Berne; Frankfurt am Main: Lang, 1985.
    ISBN 0-8204-0282-6

The publisher gratefully acknowledges the Yale University Music Library for permission to
reproduce all the illustrations in this book, with the exception of the first photograph, which
was graciously lent by Mr. Laird Kirkpatrick.

© Peter Lang Publishing, Inc., New York 1985

Printed by Lang Druck, Inc., Liebefeld/Berne (Switzerland)

To the memory of my parents

EDWIN ASBURY KIRKPATRICK (1862–1937)

and

FLORENCE CLIFFORD KIRKPATRICK (1872–1926)

and of my stepmother

ANNIS KINSMAN KIRKPATRICK (1885–1974)

Contents

Part One

EARLY YEARS

I. The Lost Paradise

Early Childhood — First Music — Our House — Books and Pictures — Echoes of Foreign Lands — My Father — My Mother — Early Disciplines — The Delicious Ordeal of Childhood — A Wedding and a Journey

I was born at about six forty in the morning of June 10, 1911, in North Leominster, Massachusetts in the south bedroom of an unbeautiful frame house at 856 Main Street into which my family had moved some years before. In a journal of my early years my mother wrote: "He was very slow about learning to control his muscles, especially those of hands and arms. At six months he used his hands hardly at all, then took a start and developed control so rapidly that he could soon equal the average child.

"He has always liked music and will listen very attentively when Marian plays and especially when she sings. When he was about twenty-five months old we noticed that he was humming the first bars of 'America.' He has always done a good deal of 'singing' but had not followed a tune before."

I was so much the youngest of the family that in many ways I received the upbringing of an only child. In 1914 when I was three years old, my elder sister, Marian (1896–1971), graduated from high school and was studying singing. My brother Clifford (1898–1971) was about to leave for Clark University in Worcester where my father had studied in 1889. My sister Alice (1902–1982) was just beginning high school. My father (1862–1937) taught psychology at what was then called Fitchburg Normal School and our lives were divided between Fitchburg, where the family had lived before my birth, and Leominster. My mother continued to go to church and to teach in the Sunday school in Fitchburg, whereas my father generally preferred the church in North Leominster.

My father was completely tonedeaf. Incapable of distinguishing one note or tune from another, he is reputed to have risen to his feet in public at the sound of *Yankee Doodle* under the impression that it was the National Anthem. But he fully understood the function of music and its meaning for others. My mother (1872–1926) had the piano lessons usually given to young girls and remained devoted to music throughout her life. I still have the mixed volumes of piano pieces (or their replacements, since from time to time they were worn to shreds) from which she played for me so frequently that I knew the precise contents of each volume, even those pieces which my mother pronounced too difficult for her. There were never any complete sonatas, but mixed among the ephemeral salon music of the last century were movements of Schubert and Beethoven. There was the E Flat Nocturne of Chopin, and the F Major *Nachtstück* of Schumann, which we also used to sing as a hymn in church. Schumann's *Aufschwung* my mother declared too difficult for her, but on my insistence she would occasionally make a stab at it. Among the salon pieces was a bit of trash called *Charm of Spring* with tinkling little chords at the extremes of the piano, which I absolutely adored. It was because of a *Skylark* of Tschaikowsky that I remember when my intimate acquaintance with these volumes was already consummated. I had noticed that grown-ups seemed to take undue pleasure in getting me to pronounce that composer's name, which I always thought sounded like sneezing. To the question concerning my age that usually accompanied this request, I frequently had occasion to reply: "I'll be four in June."

Almost as much as by the music I was fascinated by the visual appearance of the notes themselves. Long before I ever learned to read either words or music, I could identify any piece by the appearance of the notes on the page. I was susceptible to the blandness of whole- and half-notes, stimulated by quarters and eighths and thrown into a delirium by anything faster. The blackness of Chopin's *Fantasie Impromptu* gave me shivers of delighted horror. This was also a piece which my mother refused even to attempt, and I owe my first hearing of it to the grocer's daughter, a contemporary of my eldest sister, whose pudgy hands seemed to roll in billows over the keyboard as she played it. I tried imitating the movement but got a very different result. Arpeggiations were a source of endless delight and wonder, and because of them I found Rubenstein's *Kamenoi-Ostrow* profoundly gratifying. My mother was not satisfied with her performance of this piece, but I insisted on her playing it over and over again. Many years later on its account I made a special pilgrimage to that now sadly decayed suburb of Leningrad.

In these early years, apart from what I heard in church (I was devoted to the *Rosary* of Ethelbert Nevin but hated hymn singing then and ever since), the only music to which I was exposed took place at home. In addition to listening to my mother's playing, I listened intently to every new piece studied by my sisters. My eldest sister Marian had what I always considered a beautiful voice and enough facility to play her own accompaniments, but I already recognized the achievements of my other sister on the piano as less promising. My brother, who was almost as tone deaf as my father, could recognize tunes but could never sing one without transposing it three or four times within the same phrase. To the end of his life he could sometimes be overheard singing a just barely recognizable hymn tune under the bathroom shower.

Occasionally there were visiting performers, a friend of my mother's who played the Moskowski *Spanish Dances* with her in an arrangement for four hands, or the son of the local pastor who would bring his violin on a Sunday afternoon and who was never allowed to depart until at my urgent request he had played Dvořák's *Humoresque* (in G Major, of course). But the finest of the visiting performers was a bosom friend of my eldest sister who could only play one piece, the Waltz from the *Pink Lady* of Lehár, which she tossed off with a minimum of fingers and with the aplomb of a stage-hardened trouper.

Our house was scarcely distinguished enough to merit describing, but there was not a detail in it that I cannot still recall as inseparable from my other memories of childhood. It was set on about an acre and a half of flat land that evidently had been carved out of an old orchard. Eastward it looked beyond a small hill to a higher hill criss-crossed with stone walls and pastures and surmounted by an eighteenth-century farmhouse, its wellhouse and a huge barn, all of which in early morning could be seen black against the dawn, with only the gilded weathervane of the barn's cupola to herald the rising sun. Westward the back of our house looked beyond the valley of the Nashua River to the Monoosnock Hills.

Our barn was occupied by a horse, Lady, and a carriage. I think there was also a sleigh. One of my early recollections involves playing in the hay above Lady's stall, falling through the opening which led to her manger, and screaming with terror as she nuzzled at my legs. Lady was succeeded in 1915 or 1916 by an automobile, a Reo, of which I can recall only that like all other mechanical contraptions in our family it never worked very well.

Our parlor, unlike many in the neighborhood, was used for living in, for making music and for reading aloud. A reading table, magazine rack and reading chair occupied the area near the hot air register. Against the opposite wall was an upright piano with peeling imitation carving that I had to be discouraged from removing further. In front of the window to its left was a large fern in a Japanese pot on a pseudo-Oriental stand. Still further left was a rickety music cabinet surmounted by a plaster bust called *Hope.* The top two shelves were devoted not to music but to books thought to have particularly handsome bindings, for example a white and gold Keats and numerous volumes of Henry Van Dyke in dark blue and gold. The middle shelf was occupied, also not by music but by a large folio volume containing some sort of treasury of the World's Great Art. I remember especially a dead child by Bouguereau surrounded by plaster-of-Paris rosebuds, and a forlorn figure of Hope (Again! could it have been by Watts?), sunk to her knees on the top of the world and feebly clutching a broken harp. I looked at it only seldom because it always made me want to cry. The rest of the room was not particularly noteworthy, except for a few Oriental rugs agreeable to the touch as I crawled over the floor, and the stretched-out skin of a mountain lion, complete with stuffed skull from which the glass eyes had long since fallen, and over which someone was always tripping.

12

The house was furnished sparsely but unselfconsciously in the taste of the time. Nearly all the furniture was of the cheapest sort, in golden oak or imitation mahogany, with armchairs in wicker, and simple cushion-strewn cots that did duty as sofas. Most of the chairs were rockers that lacerated ankles when bumped into from the rear, and risked crushing toes when rocked forward without warning.

Electricity had only recently been installed in the house and there were no floor plugs, nor until later any table or floor lamps. For the parlor table an old-fashioned nickle-plated green-shaded kerosene lamp was considered better than electricity to read by. All the rooms and passageways on the upper floor were lit each only by one bare bulb hanging from the middle of the ceiling. In everything I have hitherto described in this house there was almost nothing, whether design, furnishings or character, that distinguished it from thousands of other rather shabby houses all over the country. What gave it distinction however was the presence of books and pictures.

My parents were inveterate self-educators. Having both grown up in pioneer families in the Middle West, they sought relief from the physical necessities and hardships of their youth, not in the pursuit of money or of luxury but in the expansion and enrichment of consciousness far beyond the confines of spelling bee and Bible class. Whereas their immediate forebears had been directed westward and forward, they were now reversing the trend eastward and backward toward the accumulated intellectual and artistic heritage of the past. Thus they unconsciously charted the pathway of my own life.

Reading was an essential part of their existence, and long before I learned to read for myself, I sensed it all around me. Part of the library was stocked with books relating to my father's work. He had been one of the first in this country to concern himself with what was called psychology. A signed photograph of William James hung over my father's desk, and together with James and many other eminences he is to be seen in the famous and often reproduced photograph that commemorates the visit to Worcester in 1909 of Dr. Sigmund Freud (to whom my sister tells me my father often referred as "Dr. Fraud"). In the library there was also a row of my father's own books, including German and Japanese translations of his best known textbook, *Fundamentals of Child Study*. For thirty years this book went through numerous editions. But all of these books, I am told, are now totally obsolete. I have never been able to make my way through a single one of them.

The library was stocked with encyclopedias, the works of major and minor English and American poets, and a rather haphazard collection of nineteenth-century fiction—Walter Scott, Dickens, George Eliot, Washington Irving, Poe, Hawthorne. Goethe and Dante were present in translation. All of this except the Goethe and the Dante I was later to devour, even to the extent of rather high-handedly appropriating certain volumes for my own library by merely writing my name on the flyleaf. There were books in the attic and in most of the bedrooms. No wonder we all ruined our eyes reading at night when we were thought to be sleeping. But all of this belongs to a much later stage of my consciousness. For the moment I was happy in knowing *Peter Rabbit* and most of the *Just-So Stories* by heart.

What attracted my attention much earlier than the books were the pictures, most of them framed photographic reproductions. The only oil painting in the house was so inept that it took me many years to discover what it was intended to represent. It probably dated from earlier years as did the enormous green photograph of moonlit waves which hung in front of the green cut-velvet stationary parlor rocker that was closest to the sources both of heat from the floor register and of light from the green-shaded kerosene lamp. Of uncertain provenance were pictures like the circular detail excepted from Rosa Bonheur's *Horse Fair* that hung in the upper front hall and those of the pre-Raphaelites such as Rossetti's *Dante at the Funeral of Beatrice* that hung behind the piano, and the *Galahad* of Burne-Jones. There were also a number of Van Dycks, and the inevitable portrait of Mme. Lebrun and her daughter.

But some of the pictures were clearly related to the recent visits of my parents to Europe, whereby they continued that trend eastward and into the past which was to become my own. They had gone separately, my mother a year before my birth and my father a year afterwards. From hearing my mother talk, I know that she visited London and the English cathedral towns (hence the large photograph of Durham Cathedral that hung in the parlor). She was in Paris (I still

14

use for bird-watching the opera glasses she bought there); in Amsterdam and Bruges; in Cologne, Heidelberg and Dresden; and in Florence and Venice. Somewhere I have the usual tourist photograph showing her feeding pigeons in front of San Marco. I wonder what she would have thought, could she have known that on the very day of her hundredth birthday, in a palace on the Grand Canal, I would be playing my first concert in Venice.

I know that my father was in Scotland (he even visited the castle of the Scottish Kirkpatricks), but I can recall no other comment of his about the rest of Europe except for Naples, by which he professed himself to be revolted. (I wonder what he would have thought of the opening chapter of my Scarlatti book.) Presumably he went to Rome but he obviously was more interested in Greece. Photographs of the Acropolis and the Parthenon hung in his library and for many years gave me the impression that the color of Greece was gray, as opposed to the sepia brown of photographs of Rome that hung in classrooms at school. He was also in Egypt and the Holy Land, from which visits he had brought back the usual trophies of scarabs real and fake, of objects made of wood from the Mount of Olives, and bits of brass from the bazaars of Damascus.

Apart from dolls, teddy bears and other animal figures I was given relatively few playthings, and most of them were designed as much to instruct as to amuse. I glimpsed some of the elementary principles of physics from the behavior of sand in the sandbox, of liquids in containers of varying sizes, of surperimposed building blocks and of rolling balls. My father did not believe in the educational benefits of mechanical toys, and I was encouraged to have as few as possible of those that ran by themselves. Thus was passed on to me his own mistrust and bafflement when confronted with machines.

Most of my father's classic psychological experiments had already been tried out on his other children, but I remember fascinating games involving recognition of sizes and shapes. All my father's last entries in the journal of my early childhood relate my exploits with the Pedometer. I became an expert at piling up the mileage by merely jumping up and down. Later I became a guinea pig for new intelligence tests, and learned ultimately to toss them off with a brilliance that stood in a most flattering relation to the real measure of my intelligence.

My father was tall, or seemed so, large-boned, blue-eyed and much better coordinated in his movements than I have ever been. Hair and moustache were already quite gray (he was forty-nine when I was born), and he seemed indeed, as in many ways he was, the model of human perfection. By the time I knew him he had achieved a remarkable inner equilibrium and an ever-increasing tolerance towards the outside world that was based on his unshakeable belief in the progress of mankind. He was seldom roused to indignation except by some particularly contemptible bit of skullduggery, and almost never lost his temper. As far as I can recall, *damn* was his only word of profanity, but that emerged only under conditions of unforeseen physical shock, like bumping his head when descending the cellar stairs. Physically he had an iron constitution, most of which I inherited, and I cannot recall his ever spending a day in bed, except once briefly after an operation for hemorrhoids. He seemed to tower serene above the ripples and billows of other people's lives. Of his own emotions he only spoke in the broadest of generalities. He seemed to have achieved a kind of monumental simplicity. As is often the case with psychologists, the fineness of his perception of the emotions of others remains an open question. Yet, whatever he may have been before I knew him, he had become and remained, even in spite of the worries and disappointments of his last years, fundamentally a happy person.

I find that I cannot say the same of my mother. By nature more volatile and impulsive than my father, she ruled herself with a will power that never relented, and her moments of weakness or discomposure were concealed from her children, except as they took the form of illness, most often sick headaches. She was like a flower that had been forced to pretend that it was made of steel. She was smaller than my father, probably less well-proportioned, and though she may have been pretty as a young girl, one now hardly thought of her as beautiful, except for the warmth of her smile and a graciousness of demeanor that made one forget any impression of a severity which she had inherited from her own mother. She was highly intelligent, perhaps more so than my father, and her mind was well-disciplined. Considering the breadth of her interests and the ability of her mind to receive and deal with information, it is suprising on opening her letters to find them correct and precise but colorless. Yet had she had occasion to publish, I think she would have written better than my father.

She was a compulsive worker, and moments of leisure (which were rare until the last years of her life) had to be useful or instructive. The housework alone, for which she had only inadequate assistance, could have been regarded as a full-time occupation. The household was lacking in nearly all the so-called modern conveniences, and the layout of the areas devoted to the preparation and serving of food could hardly have gone further in achieving the precise opposite of even the most elementary features which today are termed "labor-saving." Almost to the last she baked her own bread, always her own pastry, and at the appropriate seasons, canned, pickled and preserved large quantities of vegetables and fruit from our own garden and orchard. For years all laundry, including "flatwork," was done at home, in washtubs mounted on a folding trestle with a hand-turned wringer in the middle, and ironed with flatirons heated on the back of the kitchen range. In summer there was the flower garden to be tended, and in winter, houseplants. Always there was sewing, and housecleaning in every conceivable form. In addition to running part of the Sunday school in Fitchburg, she sang in the choral society there, and in Leominster was active in charitable organizations, the PTA and the local women's club. Yet she continued to read widely, to criticize my father's manuscripts and to take an active part in the education of her children.

In matters of discipline my father was more objective than my mother. If a spanking had to be administered he stressed the infraction of principle. My mother did likewise, so that the moral reason for any punishment was made devastatingly clear, as well as the precise nature of the recurrence it was designed to prevent, but in her case the policy of "not in anger but in sorrow" had a tendency to stress the sorrow. This meant that even the most genuine of reforms on my part were often spiced with the sting of remorse. Playthings were expected to be put away when not in use, and any left lying around were liable to temporary confiscation. If I was

17

caught telling a lie, my mouth was washed out with Ivory soap. What a privilege to have had a childhood in which one could listen without snickering to the story of George Washington and the cherry tree!

I cannot recall that I was much affected by what went on in the outside world, except as the *Just-So Stories* had opened up dimly apprehended vistas of remote ages and far countries. I was never bored; ways could always be found, either by myself or by grown-ups, of keeping me occupied or amused. There were however recurrent experiences which I hated, like having my head washed with Packer's tar soap. (To this day I loathe the smell of tar, and I am miserable in a barber's chair, whereas I fall happily asleep in that of the dentist.)

The bloody progress of the First World War seems to have impinged very little on my consciousness, except for an account in the *Youth's Home Companion* of German atrocities in Belgium illustrated (could they have been in color?) with pictures of desolated villages and flaming houses. Life inside the protected nest was too absorbing, especially as further enhanced by the preparations for my eldest sister's wedding (on June 10, 1916). They involved extended visits by the dressmaker, beautiful materials and the arrival of dazzling wedding presents. The excitement was further heightened by the prospect for my parents, my younger sister and myself of a long and distant journey. My father had agreed to exchange teaching posts for a year with a professor at the Normal School in Bellingham, Washington. We were to be absent for fourteen months. This journey was to establish my first contacts with earlier generations and with numerous relatives on both my mother's and my father's sides, all of whom lived west of the Mississippi.

II. Earlier Times and Generations

Kirkpatrick Ancestry — My Grandmother's Memoirs of Pioneering — My Father's Youth — Maternal Ancestry

Much of what had sifted through to my early consciousness about grandparents and their backgrounds was derived partly from intuition and partly from hearsay. I came to know only my maternal grandparents. About the generations prior to my great-grandparents I know very little. The Scottish name I bear, and the only non-English one in my entire ancestry, has never accurately been traced back across a gap in the mid-eighteenth century that prevents definite proof of a connection with the Kirkpatricks of Dumfrieshire and Closeburn Castle. (It was their ancestor Roger Kirkpatrick who, as an adversary stabbed by Robert Bruce lay helpless, went on to dispatch him while remarking "Ik mak' siccer." Along with the image of a bloody dagger these words were subsequently incorporated into the Kirkpatrick coat of arms.)

The earliest Kirkpatrick of my proven ancestry appears to have been in Georgia by the mid-eighteenth century. According to my grandmother's memoirs, he came from Scotland, and his son, my great-great-grandfather, was killed by Tories in the American Revolution. In Georgia, that notorious disposal ground for convicts and younger sons who had got themselves into trouble, one might find the excuse for limitless fantasies of the picaresque and disreputable. But any surviving records indicate that by the end of the eighteenth century the Kirkpatricks led lives that were both pious and respectable.

My great-grandfather Thomas Kirkpatrick left Georgia around 1800 to settle near Edwardsville, Illinois. There my grandfather Francis Asbury Kirkpatrick was born in 1815. He became a circuitriding Methodist preacher. I have the impression of a man who was moody, introspective, given to extremes of emotions and endowed with a constitution that was not of the strongest. He collected sentimental religious verse clipped out of newspapers

(I have the clippings still), and my father once told me with considerable disapproval that his father's favorite hymn was the one beginning, "There is a fountain filled with blood." Grandfather's letters reveal great uncertainties both in spelling and grammar, but these were doubtless offset in his sermons by the fervor of his delivery. There was much about him that may have provoked my father's lifelong search for enlightenment and tolerance. He appears not to have been very practical, and only in a minimal sense was he what was known as a good provider. Most of the burdens and responsibilities were assumed, with what now seems almost superhuman strength, by his wife.

My grandmother Catherine Bradbury Kirkpatrick was born "in Brown County, Ohio, September 19, 1817, near Ripley, in a large, hewed log house of two rooms." According to the memoirs she dictated to my father in 1888, her father Jacob Bradbury (my great-grandfather) was born in Massachusetts or in Maine in 1781. He

> built a boat for the family and they started to float down the Ohio in October, 1826. It was a long boat with a room and fireplace in each end, while furniture and tools were stored in the center, [he] sent the horses around by land. . . . [We] wintered near the mouth of the Ohio. . . . In going up the Mississippi, where it was rocky, they pulled the boat along with iron-pointed poles. When the wind was favorable, they sailed. . . . Landed at Naples on the 21st of March, 1827. . . . Father built two large hewed log houses with an entry between them. Cleared out about ten acres. . . . We cooked on the fireplace. Had bake oven and skillets with covers on which coals were placed. Raised cotton, wool and flax, and spun all our own clothes, but after a few years bought all but woolen goods. . . . Altogether it took nearly a day and a half to make a yard of wool cloth.
>
> Was married to Francis A. Kirkpatrick December 3, 1835. He, however, had seen me when about twelve years old out by father's home when he was passing and picked me out for his wife.

They had twelve children, of whom eleven survived to maturity. My father was the youngest. My grandmother's memoirs are too long to quote here in their entirety, but the following excerpts will give some idea of a kind of life and of a kind of fortitude of which the present-day housewife who bursts into tears at the failure of a refrigerator, or even the most aggressive women's libber, can have no conception.

Had but little to keep house with at first. Francis worked for father the first winter. He had a horse and father gave us two cows, some sheep and hogs. . . . The farm had to be grubbed out. Francis took a spell of apoplexy soon after we moved there and he had to hire the grubbing done. I sewed for people and helped lay rails. . . .

Francis was licensed to preach about a year before we came to Iowa . . . in April or May of the year 1849. . . . Francis was very successful in revivals and building up the church. He traveled on horseback and it took four weeks to make the trip. The family lived on less than $200 that year, besides what I earned sewing. The first year when we went there the parsonage was not ready and we went into another house. Francis was gone, I took sick, and they had to carry me to the wagon on a bed and move us to the parsonage. Remained there the next two years. The second year there I was very sick so that the doctor thot there was no hope for me to get well. The people at the prayer meeting prayed for my recovery and when I was in my right mind I thought of Hezekiah and prayed that fifteen years might be added to my life, that I might raise my children. [Actually she lived more than fifty years longer.]

Francis was appointed to a circuit in Louisa County about 100 miles distant and concluded to move. Teams started after him as was the custom, but it commenced raining and continued to rain so that they turned back and gave up having any minister, but in the meantime we had sold off things, so Francis hired a team to take the family (ten in all) and a few goods. He rode the horse and William drove the cows. When we got there our house was not ready. . . . The next circuit was Peoria, about one hundred miles distant. We left all our garden stuff, etc., and going to Peoria, as usual found that the house was not ready, or rather, refused us, and we had to take a poorer one. Francis received about $150 that year.

When we would have to leave a house and there seemed none to be got, Francis would be taken with the headache and could do nothing and I would have to see to everything and look out for a place to live, so those years were hard ones for me.

Later my father recalled:

When I was thirteen we had moved eighteen times. . . . When I was eight years old my mother went on a strike. She refused to get any more meals. I think she felt that father had done nothing to provide, he often left her without provision but somehow she managed.

21

This kind of life continued through my father's youth and echoes of it left their mark on my early childhood.

In 1862, the year of my father's birth, his eldest brother, my uncle William, a handsome sullen lad, was killed at Fort Donaldson in the Civil War. My grandmother writes,

> . . . William enlisted in May. . . . I told him when he started that I could only look on him as dead and he said there would be more room for the rest. He started on Sunday and came to me, asking if I would get him a drink of milk. I got some of the morning's milk. He drank part of it, but seeing how bad I felt, he could not drink the rest.

I never knew my grandmother, for she died in 1904, seven years before I was born, but throughout my childhood I felt her unseen presence. My father was her Benjamin (in 1889 he had sacrificed the pursuit of a doctorate in order to take care of her). With all she had behind her and with the difficult character that strong women develop in old age, she must have terrorized my mother as a young bride.

My father's own memoirs, while lacking the impressive conciseness of my grandmother's, continue her story and give an account of his own early youth:

> In my thirteenth year we moved to the first home of our own that I ever lived in, and the only place where up to that time I lived more than two years. . . . There were stumps of oak trees four feet in diameter not far from the house, which we used for meat blocks. . . . I never had an overcoat until I was eighteen. The only heat we had was a kitchen stove in which I built a wood fire when I got up early in the morning. Charley and I slept in the unfinished new portion of the house. In winter the sheets were decidedly cold and I usually covered up my head so that my breath would help to warm up the bed. In the morning the covers would be frozen. . . . Besides the team of ponies we always had a cow and one or more pigs and some chickens. We got all our wood from the place and soon had several acres in cultivation which furnished most of our food. . . . Much of the meat we used was obtained by shooting small game: rabbits, squirrels, quail, partridge, ducks, prairie chickens, pigeons. Sometimes we trapped rabbits or when there was a deep fresh fallen snow, we somtimes ran them down. . . . In the summertime I always preferred to go barefoot, and continued to do so until well along in my teens. . . .

He goes on to describe the experience of working as a common laborer on the construction of the Milwaukee Railroad, of working in a brickyard, of canvassing for the sale of maps and pictures and of running a drugstore.

At nineteen he was teaching in a rural school. In writing of his intellectual development he mentions buying the works of Shakespeare and Milton and the essays of Bacon and Emerson (I still have the Milton). Of his beliefs he writes:

> I was a little inclined to skepticism, but after my father's death, became a faithful believer, taking up church and Sunday School, and taking his place in family prayers. Among the few books he left was Moschine's Church History. It gave an account of the beliefs of various sects, and my conclusion after finishing this large volume, was that there was no limit to credulity, and that it was quite possible for people to hold honestly, the most absurd and contradictory beliefs.
>
> In my pre-college days I knew of no person in the neighborhood who went away to college, but I was firmly resolved that I would go sometime, even if it took me until thirty years of age to get started. An essay which I wrote in this period indicates that I firmly believed that with perseverance anything could be accomplished. There were few people of culture in the neighborhood, but I missed no opportunity to associate with people who had intellectual interests.

At the State College in Ames

> In spite of my absences and my poor preparation I finished seventh in my class, and did a good deal of work in connection with the societies and the school paper. This was possible because although I had a comparatively small amount of knowledge, yet I knew how to use my mind effectively. I think my experience in literary societies had a good deal to do with this. I was also older than most of the students, being in my twenty-second year when I entered.

After taking Bachelor's and Master's degrees at Ames College,

> . . . I was desirous of further preparation for educational work. . . . I learned that a new university was to be established at Worcester with G. Stanley Hall as president. It was to be a new type of university and the subjects of psychology and education were to be emphasized.

But he was called home in April 1888 by the illness of his mother and again the following year.

> . . . as I had become a little tired of studying without making any application of my knowledge or engaging in any practical activity of any kind, I did not go back to the university the next year. . . . I decided for the time being, at any rate, to become a minister.

But he was more interested in education than in the ministry, and in 1892 he received an appointment to teach in the State Normal School at Winona, Minnesota, where my mother became one of his students. On August 29, 1895, they were married. In 1898, the year of my brother's birth, he accepted a post at the Fitchburg Normal School in Massachusetts. This brought him back into the ambience into which I was born, which was also not far from that of my mother's forebears.

My maternal grandmother, Sarah Hale Clifford (1844–1932), was redoubtable too, but in a gentler and less all-encompassing way. She was born in Waterville, Maine, but in 1856 her father, Sherman Hale, migrated to Minnesota and finally settled near Cannon Falls where my mother was born on May 23, 1872. Grandma Clifford was short and, when I knew her, wrinkled and somewhat shrunk together. She had had a good education (in 1868 she graduated from the Winona Normal School) and was possessed of a warm and kind heart, but she was confined within the narrow bonds of a fanatical Puritanism. Throughout her life my mother corresponded with her weekly, and when my stepmother married my father, she took over the task, also later recopying my letters from abroad into a censored version fit for my grandmother's reading. My grandfather Everett Clifford (1845–1927) was a jovial sort of character who seemed to have remained relatively untouched by the severities of my grandmother. Like her, he had been born in Maine of parents who migrated to Minnesota in 1855, where the Hale and Clifford families had neighboring farms. My sisters and brother still knew his mother, Great-Grandma Clifford. I have the impression that it was she, like my Kirkpatrick grandmother, who ruled the family. Somewhere in the Clifford ancestry was a seafaring Uncle Sam, who had brought back a box of tropical shells with which I played as a child, and who had died of yellow fever in the West Indies.

My mother's parents constituted what was essentially a New England family, except as was so often the case, their Puritanism increased as they moved West, first to Minnesota and then to Oregon. They obviously enjoyed a higher standard of living and better schooling than the Kirkpatricks, but I have the impression of a tight little New England enclave transposed and concentrated, as contrasted with the free-wheeling, wide-open-space style of the Kirkpatricks. My father had much in his background that resembled that of Abraham Lincoln; some of my mother's background perhaps more resembled that of Mary Todd.

III. Growing Up

I had never before been in a Pullman car, and I regarded it with too much wonder and delight yet to assess it as one of the most devilish contrivances ever devised by man in order to ensure his own dis-comfort. Everything about it fascinated me, the green curtains, the spitoons in the washrooms, the folding tables brought out so that one might play games, the ladder on which one was assisted unstead-ily to an upper berth. Little remains in my memory of that first transcontinental trip but a few images: Lake Erie, pointed out to me by my mother in the early dawn, that seemed to have no end but the sky; crossing the Mississippi, which I already knew from my map-puzzle of the United States; a visit in Iowa with my Uncle Oliver and other relatives in towns to which I returned to play many years later when no one was left. I had never seen so much flat country.

A sojourn on a farm in Nebraska brought me my only firsthand acquaintance with the proverbial use of the corncob as an alter-native to the Sears Roebuck catalogue. (The corncob, still under-developed in Europe, was omitted by Rabelais in his exhaustive survey of those devices to which for inexplicable reasons the manu-facturers of present-day equivalents attribute "facial quality.") In the course of further visits to cousins in Denver and Colorado Springs, Pike's Peak looms in my memory too, as well as a blistering day somewhere in the desert, where while a flat tire was being repaired I sat on a very prickly cactus.

By way of Portland the family visits continued to a grand climax in Eugene, Oregon, where the descendants of two of my father's sisters constituted a staggering array of cousins in various degrees, well over a hundred.

I had noticed that my father was regarded with considerable respect by all his relatives, who were for the most part farmers. Of his generation he was by far the best educated, and the only one who had achieved recognition outside his own immediate circle. Furthermore he wrote books, a fact that conferred on him more glamor than it would now.

The bungalow of my mother's parents was situated on a small lot on the edge of Albany (Oregon) and looked out over land that was not yet built up and distinguished only by its unremitting flatness and its capacity for attracting and retaining heat in the summer. My grandparents had retired there in order to be near my mother's only brother, Uncle Clarence.

We spent both the summers of 1916 and 1917 in Albany, during which I was introduced by my cousins to the wonderful world of the Oz books. At Chautauqua I was frightened out of my wits by a speaker who told us we were all damned and would go to Hell. *Pilgrim's Progress*, read to me by my grandmother, was one of the most odious literary experiences of my life. Churchgoing and the observance of the Sabbath were stricter than anything I had known at home. Forty-five years later, without guidance, I was able to identify the Presbyterian church where I had first heard the hymn "Faith of our Fathers."

During one of these summers, while watching my grandfather chop kindling I made an unexpected movement, and his hatchet sank itself into the second finger of my left hand, where I still bear the scar. Had the hatchet gone half an inch further, the entire course of my subsequent life would have been changed. But the most exciting event of the summer of 1916 was the sudden arrival of my eldest sister Marian, who brought me a little purple glass dog with rhinestone eyes. For reasons which I did not understand at the time, but which for once were not her fault, she had left her husband

and had come to join us. The marriage had lasted less than two months.

The Normal School at Bellingham, and not far from it our house, was situated on middle ground of the slope that rises from Puget Sound in the West to Mount Chuckanut in the East. Huge tree stumps from the primeval forest were still in evidence here and there, and all the sidewalks were of wood. Over Puget Sound, with the snow-covered Olympics sparkling in the North, could be observed at dusk some of the most magnificent sunsets I have ever seen, and at night the flames of burning residue from the sawmills. I have never returned to Bellingham, but despite the mild climate this sojourn in the Pacific Northwest gave me a feeling of Northness, of contact with remote regions that I had never before sensed. It may have been here that my mother first pointed out to me the *Aurora Borealis*. But I have fond and definite memories of a confection called a *North Pole* by the local ice cream parlor. In the center of a mound of snowy ice cream stood a red and white peppermint stick surmounted by a glowing Maraschino cherry.

My sister Marian resumed the study of the piano, and I envied her the *Scarf Dance* of Chaminade and something else called *The Flatterer* because it was nearly all on the black keys and began each brace with a tangle of flats to indicate the key of G-flat. I have no recollection of Wilson's declaration of war, but before the end of April 1917 we got the news that my brother had enlisted to go to France as an ambulance driver.

After a second summer with my grandparents in Albany there was another fling in Eugene with the "cousins by the dozens" and a sojourn in tents on the slopes of Mount Rainier just above tree line among abundant wildflowers and icy streams. We went East by way of the Canadian Rockies and broke the further journey by a visit to my mother's birthplace, an unprepossessing little white farmhouse in the middle of flat country.

Shortly after our return, my mother fulfilled her promise of allowing me to begin study of the piano. For the first year she taught me herself. Later I was given lessons by Mrs. Fanny Richardson, the organist of the North Leominster church. I remember little about the lessons, but in church I became accustomed to hearing her accompany the clatter of coins in collection plates with such pieces as the *Last Hope* and the Sextet from *Lucia*. Instead of sending me to school, my mother covered the work of the first two grades in one year by tutoring me at home.

The rhythms of the household reestablished themselves much as they had been before our departure for the West. Sundays, while increasingly secularized, maintained a certain ritual quality that persisted throughout the years. In the morning before church my father polished the shoes of the whole family. We then dispersed to our respective churches in Fitchburg and North Leominster. I was taken to one or the other, but I think principally in the early years to the Fitchburg church so that I might go to Sunday school. There the principal activities that I remember consisted in pasting little stickers into attendance books and marching, rather pointlessly it seemed, from one room of the parish house to another while a Mrs. Taylor played a battered upright piano. One of our classrooms had black horsehair furniture on which one could never keep from sliding and which in worn spots pricked and tickled in a most disagreeable way. We learned the names and sequence of the books of the Bible, and to this day I can reel off the names of the Minor Prophets in three and one-half seconds flat.

Sunday dinner, to which we returned late on the trolley car from Fitchburg, was usually cooked by my eldest sister, who had sung somewhere in church but returned earlier than those of us who had Sunday school. In the afternoon we usually went for a walk in the still unspoiled countryside, often to the top of the hill facing our house, from where we could see Mount Wachusett and on a clear day even Monadnock. In the later afternoon friends came to call, often my future stepmother Annis Kinsman and her sister Grace. At about six in the evening my father disappeared into the kitchen and could be heard shaking the cornpopper over the stove. After the ritual of popcorn in the parlor, which was almost never missed, the family dispersed into the kitchen for what was known as a "stand-up supper," consisting generally of various leftovers extracted from the icebox.

Apart from the cultivation of the garden and fruit trees and from the ordinary household tasks, there were hideous upsets produced by the waxing of floors or by paperhanging and painting. There were also summer expeditions to Wachusett, where whole days were spent gathering blueberries that afterwards were to be made into endless muffins, shortcakes, pies and preserves. Such haying as could not be negotiated by my father with a scythe was done by a horse-drawn mowing machine driven by a small wiry woman of indeterminate age in pants and short hair who also did the plowing and the carting of dirt and manure for the garden, delivered the milk, and took charge of the drowning of unwanted kittens and the castration of tom-cats.

The war fever was mounting to a high pitch, and we anxiously awaited my brother's letters. Often they arrived in shreds, with great patches clipped away by the censors. One heard talk of the Huns, of the Boches, and of the big German drive expected for the spring of 1918. Much was made of German atrocities in Belgium and France, and not long afterward I tacked on the wall of my room a triple photograph of Rheims Cathedral as it looked before, during and after its bombardment. Everyone was knitting something in khaki-colored wool—socks, leggings, sweaters, caps and mufflers—and we children were mobilized to collect nutshells for the making of charcoal to put in gas masks.

At the Armistice there was rejoicing such as never has been seen for the end of any subsequent war. At the first premature news, the bell of the North Leominster church was rung so violently that its rope broke and it could not be used to celebrate the confirmation of the real Armistice. We children paraded up and down the street with signs hung on our little carts that read, "To Hell with the Kaiser." In June 1919 my brother returned decorated and disillusioned. He was not to go back to Europe until the time of Hitler's ascendancy, and again at the end of the Second World War when he was sent on a mission measuring the effect on the civilian population of the bombings in Germany. These experiences scarcely alleviated the despair and pessimism which he had never lost since his own experience of war. My father however seemed always to have kept his faith in the progress and perfectibility of mankind.

Meanwhile my sister Alice had gone off to Middlebury College as a freshman in September 1918 and I had entered school for the first time. It is at this point that what I think of as a happy childhood ends. Although my family was in excellent social and civic relations with all neighbors, my parents had few intimate friends, and I am not sure that in both their cases their own reserve did not place distinct limits on any degree of intimacy. I cannot recall a reference by either of my parents to anyone of their own generation by first name, no matter how long-standing or how close the friendship. Only those who definitely qualified as members of the younger generation were addressed or referred to by their first names. For my own part, I had few contemporaries who had anything in common with my own background. With few exceptions my isolation and the consequences of it were to increase throughout my school days.

In early 1919, on the bow-legged old square piano in the parish house of the North Leominster church I played as my first public performance an inane little piece in E-flat called *Bitte* by a composer whose name I have long forgotten. Shortly before this my mother had begun to take me to concerts. One was a very patriotically oriented performance by the soprano Marcella Craft in January 1919, but a pencil scrawl in what must be my earliest hand indicates that earlier I had heard Mabel Garrison at the Fitchburg Normal School. This inscription appears at the beginning of a notebook on the outside of which I had pasted a rotogravure photograph of the singer Amelita Galli-Curci, and in which I mounted the programs of all the concerts I heard. I continued this practice in later notebooks until my graduation from Harvard. They give an almost complete record of the music which I heard in public performance for twelve important years. In March 1919 I was taken to hear Galli-Curci herself, whom I was led to regard as "the greatest singer in the world," and in November and December to two concerts which in after years I remembered as having been my first, one by the Flonzaley Quartet and the other by Harold Bauer and Jacques Thibaud. Several times I was taken to hear Sousa's band and the two-piano team of Maier and Pattison. Every spring the Fitchburg Choral Society presented a festival with imported orchestra and soloists, sponsored by a music-loving local paper manufacturer. There, between 1919 and 1922, among oratorios by Coleridge-Taylor, Gounod and César Franck, I heard such works as the *Damnation of Faust* of

31

Berlioz, the Rossini *Stabat Mater* and the Verdi *Requiem*.

At some time during the winter of 1919 and 1920 we were persuaded to buy a phonograph. Known as a Columbia Graphophone, it was a huge affair like an overgrown pedestal desk perched on claw feet, with a drawer at one end for the turntable and with the speaker at the other. Below there were bins for storing records. The whole was surmounted by a thick plate-glass top which protected its red mahogany veneer. This piece of furniture replaced the old reading table, and the light now came from an electric lamp in metal and Tiffany-like glass. The records were played with fiber needles that had to be sharpened between each selection. They were thick and grooved only on one side. Most of them were vocal, since piano music was still considered not to record well, chamber music unpopular, and large orchestral works quite out of the question. There was Galli-Curci with the flute in one of her coloratura airs, John McCormick singing *Una furtiva lagrima*, Mary Garden in *Depuis le jour*, Ernestine Schumann-Heink like a foghorn belting out *Vom Himmel Hoch*, Louise Homer in a rather prim *Mon Coeur s'ouvre à ta voix*, and a star-studded *Rigoletto* quartet. There were a few violin salon pieces by Heifetz, Kreisler and Maud Powell, but the only piece of symphonic literature that I recall was the slow movement of Beethoven's Fifth Symphony conducted by Walter Damrosch.

The principal orientation of our record collection, like that of the Victor and Columbia catalogues which I studied with avidity and from which I clipped photos and blurbs for my scrapbook, was toward opera. After my brother had given me the *Victrola Book of the Opera* for Christmas, my obsession knew no bounds. I read and re-read the stories of the operas, from *L'Africaine* straight through to *Zaza* and looked again and again at the photographs of robust divas against the musty scenery of great opera houses. After a visit to Fitchburg had been announced by a barn-storming opera troupe I slept for a week with the tickets under my pillow, only to be bitterly disappointed when the performance was cancelled because of a blizzard. (Some fifty-four years later I finally heard and saw *Il Trovatore* for the first time in a superb performance at the freshly resuscitated Paris Opera.) My room was lined with pictures of composers. On being given a subscription to *Musical America* I devoured with gusto all its blurbs and gush, and I was deeply moved by the deaths in 1921 of Saint-Saëns and Caruso.

After about a year of Mrs. Richardson's piano lessons, my mother, who closely supervised both lessons and practice, must have decided that it was time for me to move on. Miss Elizabeth Perry, supervisor of music at the Fitchburg Normal School, was persuaded to take me over. With her I studied many Mozart sonatas, but how I played such works as the late Fantasy and Sonata in C-minor or the composite sonata in F-major I cannot imagine. However, Mozart had permeated my consciousness and I used to make up and whistle Mozart-like melodies while walking home from school. It was with Miss Perry that I studied my first Chopin, the G-major nocturne opus 37 No. 2, and the *Tarantelle* of which latter I gave what everyone thought an electrifying performance for the North Leominster PTA on the old golden oak upright piano of my seventh grade classroom. It was about the time of my eleventh birthday.

When Miss Perry went away for a sabbatical in 1922, she turned me over to Miss Vera Johnson in Leominster, a one-time pupil of Harold Bauer. Miss Johnson talked much about piano touch, and in one of her weekly assignment books I find a list of the eight or ten different piano touches (I no longer understand what she meant by any of them). Apparently she also began by giving me stretching exercises which ended by increasing to the utmost the extension of my already large hands. As a result I can trill in octaves in either hand, a capacity for which I found no musical employment until 1960, when at my request Henry Cowell put such a trill in the bass of a piece he was writing for me. In 1922, when I was eleven, and for some years thereafter, I could bend any finger backwards far enough to touch the top of my forearm.

A letter of my mother's to my grandmother records a joint recital on June 19, 1923, with Jacob Cohen, the son of a local cobbler, who afterwards preceded me to Harvard but who subsequently gave up the piano altogether. He played the flashy pieces. My contributions were confined to a modest transcription of a Bach Bourrée from one of the cello suites, the Andante from the *Pathétique* of Beethoven, *Country Gardens* of Percy Grainger (*my* warhorse!) and *A Day in*

Venice of Ethelbert Nevin. As a finale we played together the *Second Hungarian Rhapsody* of Liszt arranged for four hands.

In the same month I finished grammar school and graduated from the eighth grade. It was the end of my childhood and the moment when many problems that had long been preparing themselves were about to emerge. At school, except by a handful of tolerant and loyal friends, from one year to another I was more and more bullied and teased, with the result that increasingly I withdrew into the world of reading and of music. But my conception of music was that of an amusement, not of a discipline, and my mother and Miss Johnson tried their best to keep me in paths that would permit progress.

Furthermore, things were not going too well for my sisters and brother, and their influence, or perhaps rather that of their lives, began to play an increasing part in shaping my character. My eldest sister Marian, who had gone to New York in the ill-founded hope of making a career as a singer, had returned in 1921 beaten and broken by a series of unhappy love affairs and by the inadequacies of her preparation, either in accomplishment or perseverance, to make her way in New York.

If I have said little about my younger sister Alice, it is because Marian's flamboyance overshadowed all the other members of the family. She had rebelled against the intellectualism in which all the rest of us took refuge, but her search for freedom was continually thwarted by the background against which it took place, and probably also by my mother's tacit disapproval. She had a good mind, but it went untrained and her judgment in human affairs was poor. She was capable of totally ignoring certain generally accepted rules of conduct, such as that of not reading other people's letters. What was worse, she talked about them afterwards, and her indiscretion was such that all the rest of us early developed habits of secrecy, especially about those things things that mattered to us most. She was generous and outgoing, and wanted to be loved, but all her life she displayed an uncanny knack for wounding the innermost sensibilities of others through carelessness and indiscretion, and for probing the wound until she made herself unbearable. She was attractive and made friends easily, but was incapable of keeping any of them except for a few intimates of her youth. My brother escaped many of her worst influences, but when he was on his deathbed he refused to read her letters.

My sister Alice, thwarted by Marian's virtual monopoly on such perquisites of femininity as beauty, grace and easy attractiveness to men, and revolted by her instabilities, took refuge in outdoor pursuits and in the cultivation of the mind, but she too had her difficulties and came home before the end of her junior year at Middlebury with the equivalent of a mild nervous breakdown. It was then that she and I both fell into the hands of the orthopedist. Curved spines and fallen arches were diagnosed and measures prescribed for rectifying them. I was given some sort of hideously uncomfortable brace to hold my back straight, and a pair of black-enamelled iron arch supports which revealed an extraordinary capacity for raising blisters. I cannot recall how I got rid of the brace, but I well remember burying the arch supports one day behind the rhubarb patch in the vegetable garden, long before they could have possibly filled their intended function. Yet for many years I have never displayed the slightest trace of flat feet.

After his return from the war, my brother Clifford was seldom at home, and the background of his childhood was so different from mine that in later life it almost seemed as if we had grown up in different families. It was only after my mind began to develop that we established any sort of give and take of communication. He was devastatingly logical and gifted with the sharpest powers of analysis, of which he made use to puncture many an illusion, whether religious, moral or esthetic. Quite early in his graduate studies he had abandoned chemistry in favor of sociology. He adored my father, and between them there was endless shop talk, interspersed with games of tennis. My brother had little of the New Englander in him, except for a dark strain of pessimism which I always suspected he had inherited from our maternal grandmother. Because of his championing of new and liberal ideas, he never recognized that far more than I he was a Puritan in reverse. Externally and in life style he reverted to the middle west of my parents. He had little use for small talk, and his conversation nearly always turned to the materials and measurements of his researches. Despite his exceptional intelligence, in both talking and writing he was a veritable fountain-head of sociological jargon. After I had developed in a quite different direction, I often teased him about his substitution of jargon for English, until I came to see that I was in danger of hurting his feelings.

His early influence on me was twofold. On the one hand, his pessimism and the destructive techniques of analysis that disguised themselves under what he sincerely believed to be objectivity, seen in the light of the unacceptable examples furnished me by the behavior of my eldest sister, brought out in me an untimely cynicism and mistrustfulness. On the other hand, the stimulus of his intellect helped me to articulate my own, to emulate a rigor that was not always present in my father's thinking, and to couple it with my father's belief that "with perseverance anything could be accomplished."

But more than I realized at the time, the clouds were gathering around me. Already my trust in human relations had been severely shaken by my sister's instabilities and failures and by my own experiences at school. My faith in religion and in moral principles had been undermined by my brother's bitterness and disillusionment. Church-going had become desperately boring, not only because of the sermons and the seemingly blind respect accorded Bible texts, but also because of the unsatisfying quality of the music that I heard there. My father had made an agreement with me that I would continue church-going until my twelfth birthday, after which I would be free to choose as I liked. From that day on I rarely went to church, and if in later years I suffered through innumerable sermons it was only because I needed the money earned by singing in the choir. In July 1923, at the age of twelve I became an atheist.

I find myself wondering what, despite my loss of faith in human relations and in religious principles, at this point can have held me together. I think it was probably the stability provided by my parents, for whom I had unqualified admiration; along with the unfailing pleasures provided by music and reading; and a belief in what was supposedly rational thinking and decent behavior, which despite his disillusionment my brother had himself never lost. In another context I would doubtless have gone the way of the disoriented and uprooted youth of fifty years later. At any rate, I had already acquired many of the distortions that never again could be eliminated, and that could only be counterbalanced by the development of other elements in my character.

In the autumn of 1922 I entered high school. The next four years of my life are those which I would least prefer to live over again. Although I was still surrounded by a small group of faithful and even intimate friends, my isolation from the general run of my contemporaries only increased. With a few exceptions I had no further contact in later life with these schoolmates, nor for the most part did I desire it. The only one with whom I have always remained in touch is the North Leominster pastor's grandson, the mathematician Saunders MacLane. After the death of his father, his mother had brought him and his two brothers to live with their grandfather, who was a man highly respected by all my family for his outstanding character and intelligence. His daughter-in-law was gentle, gracious and also highly intelligent. She was one of those who sat with me when my mother died, and to the end of her life she was a devoted friend of my stepmother. Like most of the males in his family Saunders began by playing the violin, but I seem to have recollections of caterwaulings that revealed an almost total absence of talent for the arts. However, along with my brother he had the most brilliant mind of any of the persons I frequented during these years.

In high school I was exposed to some very good teaching, especially in English grammar and composition, but despite all good intentions of teachers, certain classics like Shakespeare and Milton were rendered unreadable for me until long afterward. I achieved a fairly adequate reading knowledge of French, but my study of Latin resulted in an inability today to read even a single verse of Horace or Virgil or to decipher the simplest tombstone. Mathematics was a lost cause, and though I have retained the multiplication table and can add and subtract if I concentrate intensely, I no longer have the faintest idea how to do long division or to extract a square root. For years I have said, probably unjustly, that the greatest benefit that I derived from high school was learning to type.

Reading as always was an immense preoccupation and solace. Long before the end of grammar school I had devoured all the children's books handed down from my elders. Later I read most of the fiction in the family library: Walter Scott, Dickens, Poe, Hawthorne, Thackeray. But I resented being made to cry by *Old Curiosity Shop* or by the end of *Uncle Tom's Cabin*, feeling that somehow their authors were taking unfair advantage of me. I think that I have always been a little suspicious of facile pathos and inclined to demand a less sentimental but broader view. Many current books were read aloud at home, for example, the *Education of Henry Adams* and the ineffably smug *Autobiography of Edward Bok*. It must have been at about this time that I read the *Outline of History* by H.G. Wells from cover to cover. The limited resources of the family library and budget were admirably supplemented by the Leominster Public Library. Almost anything worth reading seemed to be available, whether classics or current books, and I probably owe more of my education to that library than to my formal schooling. For this reason I have always felt an interest in any public library. I believe that anyone who so wishes can get an education there and that such libraries remain our strongest bastions of human dignity and freedom.

After graduating from Middlebury in 1922 Alice spent a year at home before embarking on the study and later the profession of librarianship, bringing with her echoes of her college experience, especially literary and esthetic. She also initiated a wave of decorative reform which spread through the house, conferring on it a self-consciousness which it never again lost. Color schemes, never previously mentioned, were now subjects of conversation, and my mother was encouraged to luxuries which she had never before permitted herself. My mother had always raised flowers, and my sister now encouraged her further. All of this interested me to a degree quite disproportionate for one of my age. I also became aware of what was known as "antiques," and I admired the houses of the eighteenth century and made the acquaintance of local historians.

Meanwhile music continued to be my dominant interest, more and more the romantic composers. I had forgotten Mozart except for a few of Zerlina's and Susanna's arias which my sister sang, and until many years later I disliked Beethoven. My wholehearted devotion went to Chopin, Schumann, Liszt and their imitators. In November 1922 I had been taken to Worcester to hear Paderewski in one of the first concerts he played after coming out of retirement. Above all I remember the waving of his long golden hair as he bounded onto the platform and my rapture when he played the G-major Nocturne, the first piece of Chopin that I had ever played myself. Paderewski played long programs. I have this one in front of me, and it lists some of the greatest works in all piano literature, but they must have gone straight over my head. He played the *Variations Sérieuses* of Mendelssohn; the Schumann *Fantasy*; the *Appassionata* of Beethoven; a group of four Chopin pieces including the *Nocturne*, the G-minor *Ballade* and the C-sharp minor *Scherzo*; and finally three pieces of Liszt, none of them short. This was topped off by the usual encores. A year later I was taken to Boston to hear De Pachmann, about whom I remember little but his eccentricities.

But in November 1923, under circumstances for which I have no way of accounting, Rachmaninoff came to play in the City Hall in Leominster. He played part of an English Suite of Bach and the *Variations Sérieuses* of Mendelssohn, which this time I remember, and two pieces that absolutely bowled me over, the C-sharp minor *Scherzo* of Chopin by which I had been previously unmoved, and *Funérailles* of Liszt. Among the encores was his own inevitable and fervently-hoped-for *Prelude* in C-sharp minor. Another performance that transported me was that of Olga Samaroff in the 1919 spring festival of the Fitchburg Choral Society when she played the Chopin A-flat *Ballade* and the *Twelfth Hungarian Rhapsody* of Liszt.

My own piano repertoire and my facility were expanding, but more than ever my mother found it necessary to supervise my practicing and to attend my lessons. To the best of my ability I resisted every form of systematic discipline, and my mother was rewarded for her perseverance by some terrible scenes. Occasionally however, but all too infrequently, she was able to take pleasure in the evidence of at least partial success of her efforts. In her diary for 1924 she records a few of these satisfactions: "Went to Fortnightly Club Social in P.M. Ralph played *To Spring* by Grieg, *Autumn* by McDowell. Did very well. Many compliments." On March 16 she mentions one of the evenings when my father read aloud his favorite passages from the book of *Ecclesiastes*: "R's music in background. Fine effect." But on April 16 she makes a negative report: "Ralph's music lesson not a success. He worked last week but not by correct methods. Have not supervised lately." However in June 1924 I played in a recital of Miss Johnson's pupils a *Romance* of Sibelius, with great fervor I am sure, because I have always had a predilection for the tactile sensations of piano pieces in D-flat and related keys. The recital terminated with the *William Tell Overture*, played four hands by "Masters Cohen and Kirkpatrick."

By now adolescence had begun to manifest itself in all its most unattractive forms. I was moody, rebellious, inarticulate and increasingly difficult to manage. I think I made little trouble for my father, but on my mother fell the whole brunt of maintaining daily discipline, especially that of practicing and of performing household duties. She insisted that I be responsible for the maintenance of order and cleanliness in my own rooms. Furthermore, she insisted that I learn most of the techniques of housekeeping, including the pressing of suits and even the ironing of shirts. (This latter is a skill that I admit as rarely as possible to ever having possessed.) The constant pressures that she felt obliged to bring upon me made it almost completely impossible for her to relax in my presence, and in any case she had long since disciplined herself against facile displays of affection. The result was that I came more and more to frequent adult friends and households which would offer me a welcome that was all the more demonstrative for being free of the embarrassing and perplexing task of bringing me up. Among such households were those of parents of my contemporaries, of my antique-collecting adult friends and that of my future stepmother and her sister where I had always been welcome since childhood. My mother in no way begrudged me these frequentations of other households, but on one occasion when I had gone off leaving once again my assigned duties unperformed she must have felt that the time had come to summon me rather peremptorily home. Upon arriving, I made a scene such as never before or since. It was probably the ugliest manifestation of my entire adolescent years. She left a note under my door which I never forgot, although fifty years had to pass before I could bring myself to open it again.

She wrote:

Dear Ralph,

In order to correct if possible your very evident misunderstanding of my motive in calling you home this afternoon, I should explain that I don't consider the matter of a few inches, more or less of dirt on a floor, a question of supreme importance and if it were merely a matter of consulting one's own taste, a wardrobe gracefully distributed over the floor is of course as good as one hung in the conventional fashion. When you have an establishment of your own, such innovations will be entirely in order and no one's business but your own.

As long as you have a room in an establishment of which you are not the head, but in which as being your home, you have a profound interest, it would seem the part of courtesy to observe the ordinary rules of behavior and room order.

What *does* concern me, as being of great importance in this character forming stage of your life, is the tendency to disregard or put off indefinitely the few duties for which you are held responsible. You will have to make your own living sometime and the greatest asset you can have in that difficult task is the reputation for promptness and reliability. A habit of calling your parents unpleasant names when their actions do not please you will not get you anything desirable. A good many people have a prejudice against that way of showing one's feeling of self importance.

You and I have so many tastes in common that our relations ought to be very pleasant but such a scene as that this afternoon makes me feel that I should be glad not to see another sunrise.

I think that if you consider the matter carefully you will feel that I am not unreasonable in thinking that you owe me an apology either written or oral for your language.

Probably you will be no more inclined to believe it than you are to believe other things that older people say but your mother really has your best interests and happiness much at heart, and only wishes that you could see some things as clearly now as you will in later years.

Lovingly
Mother

In January 1926 I went for the last time to a concert with my mother. It was a recital in Boston by Harold Bauer. On February 23 she left for Oregon to visit her parents. Postcards arrived from her on the way, and finally one from her destination saying that she was very tired and not feeling well. On March 10 I began the following letter:

Dear Mother,
We got your card today; sorry to hear you aren't feeling well. The piano tuner has just left and the piano sounds marvelous. You'll love my new Chopin Impromptu [in F-sharp major]. It sounds exactly as the bells used to on Sunday mornings in spring, with just the same fresh sweetness of new leaves and apple blossoms. Incidentally it is hard, one section with octaves in the left hand and trying to break the broad-jump record. There are four pages of runs to be covered in about hald a minute, and touch work everywhere. I'm expecting Miss Johnson any minute for my lesson. The sun is shining in here slantways, almost like summer. It thaws in the daytime and freezes again at night, so you can imagine the condition of the roads!

I have worked a new plan of going to bed at eight and rising to practice before school. So now I see the sunrises, which are gorgeous. Yesterday morning everything was purple and lavender, from the sky and the snow to my furniture.

Before I had finished my letter, which was never sent, a telegram arrived from my uncle saying that my mother was seriously ill with uremic poisoning and that my father had better come at once. She died on March 22. Life had worn her out.

A dream that recurs even to this day has it that she did not die at all, but was only away, "elsewhere." She has returned, but is strangely distant and reserved. I am about to try to acquaint her with some of what in the meantime has happened when I awaken, often in tears.

From this moment I began growing up rapidly. Heightened perceptions and sensibilities were accompanied by searches for ultimate truths. In a long conversation with Saunders MacLane, who, although I don't think he believed a word of it, kept the argument on the strictest paths of logical discourse, I concluded that Beauty was All. My sister Alice further encouraged my esthetic pursuits in the direction of literature, poetry, interior decoration and the observation of Nature. Furthermore, we banded together for protection against the aggressions of my sister Marian and in reaction to the banality of the life she was leading with her second and last and soon-to-be-divorced husband. I took over the care of my mother's garden and became an expert on the planting and seasonal planning of mixed perennial borders. At moments, fortunately brief, I even thought of becoming an interior decorator or a landscape gardener! Boston represented the natural center of all my interests. It was for me the great metropolis, and my increasingly frequent excursions there never failed to be exciting and rewarding.

At about the time I was preparing to emerge from adolescence and became a person I had read Emerson on *Self-Reliance*. From then on I practiced self-reliance with a vengeance. It healed some of the wounds of my isolation, but above all it persuaded me that I could take many matters under my own control and gave me courage to do so. I have been an incurable do-it-yourselfer ever since. I learned to make use of solitude, even to require it for certain periods of time. While the mouse-trap theory hardly takes into account today's problems of marketing and distribution, I still believe that if one does something well enough it will make its way. Even if the whole world has not beaten a path to my door, the way has become well enough known to enable me to go on doing the very work I most wanted to do.

But there are dangers, those of losing contact, and what my sociologist brother used to call "interaction," with much of the outside world. One of my English teachers, a very wise lady from Chicago, saw them in my case and tried to warn me. Fortunately much of what she foresaw was averted by the circumstances of my subsequent life, but nevertheless a heavy price has been paid for my habits of independence, and doubtless there is more still to pay.

In his dealings with me my father took the wisest possible course, that of refraining from pressures that would have produced outright opposition on my part. With nothing to react against, I became all the more conscious of my own responsibilities. He encouraged me in all my interests, even in those such as music of which he had no understanding, and left to me not only the day-to-day decisions but also those concerning my future.

I spent hours at the piano, and not only dealt with most of the great warhorses of piano literature but also explored new music brought back from Boston, especially Debussy and Ravel. Never had a pupil of Miss Johnson's played such a wide range of music. My facility had so increased that I could sightread anything, though not always with due regard for details, and often with even less regard for the rhythm. I dealt with technical problems more by faking than by solving them. Almost nothing was fit for performance, and when occasions arose for playing in public, even I knew enough to fall back on pieces that made only limited technical demands. Nevertheless I had notions at times of becoming a concert pianist. Fortunately there was no one near me who would have been foolish enough to urge me into taking the disastrous course of entering a conservatory. My other interests were so great that it was not at all difficult for me to decide that I wished to go to Harvard.

In June 1927 I played *Aufschwung* of Schumann in the Leominster City Hall at the graduation exercises of the high school. Never again have I gone near Leominster High School, not even within sight of it.

In May 1927 my father married our family friend Annis Kinsman. I had known her ever since I could remember, and practically as soon as I could toddle I had been welcome at her father's house. He was a redoubtable old gentleman, twice widowed, who had retired to his birthplace after a career in electronics. I well remember sitting on his knee and joking with him in the sunlit bay window of his study. Mr. Kinsman had put all the suitors of his daughters to flight, and even when the daughters were in their thirties they professed to be terrorized by him. But their later lives showed that they were made of quite as strong stuff as he. For years, however, the end of their Sunday afternoon visits to our house had been announced by the exclamation, "We must be getting home or Father will have a fit!" Annis (throughout her life, probably because of her outgoing ways, she was nearly always called by her first name) had taken up librarianship in 1916 and came home only for weekends. Her younger sister Grace sang, in a pleasing but exceedingly light soprano. One of her specialties, as I recall, was "When Dawn Breaks in the Sky. . . ." Her health was delicate, and her attempts at careers in various directions were generally interrupted by long stays at home, where, like her sister, she was always ready for fun with younger people.

Annis, now my stepmother, continued the tactic she had always taken with me, which was also my father's, of giving me a maximum of encouragement with a minimum of censure. To the best of her abilities, for she hated housekeeping, she took over my mother's garden and household duties, but she had stood up to her own father too often, and had experienced too much independence to knuckle under without protest in a ready-made situation, as my mother had done as a young bride. My father's aloofness baffled her, and just because she adored him she tried constantly to get him to descend from his pedestal. The atmosphere of stoical resignation and simulated calm that had prevailed in my mother's lifetime was now animated in a way that inevitably brought about frictions and, in my opinion, inconsiderate behavior on the part of my sisters and brother. But she forgave them all and after my father's death did her best to act as he would have wished. Although she freely expressed her opinions of people in a way that my mother had never permitted herself, her discretion in confidential matters was iron-bound, and never did she burden me with a tactless question or comment. Sensing the imminent end of her long life and wishing to express my gratitude to her before it should be too late, I wrote in 1973 as follows:

> . . . our friendship of some sixty years (at any rate as long as I can remember) has meant more to me than any other in my life. . . . From the beginning, when as a child I used to visit your house, or later when you and Grace came to call on Sunday afternoons, and above all in the years since you entered the family, your affection, confidence, sympathy, discretion, comfort and encouragement have been for me a constant source of strength and reassurance. . . .

During my father's lifetime all the members of my family remained in contact through correspondence and holiday meetings even though the divergences in background and interests were becoming more and more apparent. But after my father's death we never came together at the same time until a reunion that I organized in 1962. We were all so totally different in temperament and in appearance that casual acquaintances were always astonished to learn that we had all come from the same brood.

My brother remained closer to my father than I, so much did their common interests furnish inexhaustible material for conversation. My interests had swung into directions that were unfamiliar if not inaccessible to my father, and our relationship was more distant, but marked by a certain amount of satisfaction on his part and by an unfailing respect on mine. One of his last pleasures was the simultaneous and unprecedented award in 1936 to my brother and myself of Guggenheim fellowships. On January 4, 1937, a coronary thrombosis carried away my father in his sleep. A quarter-century later I was moved to address an imaginary letter to him:

September 29, 1962

Dear Father,

On the occasion of your hundredth birthday, I am wondering how to write to you. You have been dead for twenty-five years, and I am not sure that you still exist otherwise than in the consicousness of those who have known you or in the unconscious influences you continue to exert. Yet you yourself were so completely accepting of the total courses of life and history (you once said death was merely a part of the great life-process), that however voluntarily you may have been absorbed by them, I feel justified in addressing you in the same way that I would always have done, that a concept of you exists that makes it seem as if I might stamp and mail this letter to you, as I might have done when you were alive.

. . .

You and I were never very close, nor would we be now. Much would always have to remain unsaid. Many of our interests would always lie in different fields, and many of our esthetic and critical judgments would have no hope of meeting, even on the common ground of argument. I do not have confidence in the penetration or the acuity of many of your perceptions. Yet to this day I cannot discover a human quality in you, an aspect of character, that I do not find completely admirable. I am aware of no dark corners, of no unreliabilities, of nothing that is not competely clean and worthy of emulation. The vision of honesty and integrity that you left with us was also a reality.

Any moral fiber, any remnant of purity that remains to my twisted and corrupted nature, harks back to this vision. Notions of independence, self-reliance, fair dealing, respect of the autonomy and integrity of others, conceptions of patience, all have this origin. It is relatively unimportant

46

that I should find it impossible to accept all of your optimism, all of your generation's hopes of human perfectibility. That your philosophy apparently chose to ignore aspects of human nature and history that we now consider unavoidable may have diminished the stature and durability of some of your teachings, but not of your person. You were the goodly, beautiful, temperate, somewhat inaccessible, kindly man who might easily have been thought to be the embodiment of an ideal.

Is it not then worthwhile to have lived, to have conferred on children and onlookers the vision I have just described? Though each generation brings increasing forgetfulness, where do the influences ever stop? When can the effect of the last concentric ripple of the water-thrown stone be said to cease?

Let me mention a few of the ways in which I am able to see that your influence is still attributably active. It permeates every moment of my teaching with a belief in the cultivation of considered individual judgment, in the capacity of the individual to enlarge his own perceptions and horizons, in conceptions of reasonableness, of the orderly arrangement of ideas and working processes, in the superiority of personal initiative to externally enforced discipline. Your influence has given me the belief that any technique can be acquired, any area of knowledge explored, if the individual really so wishes. It was undoubtedly you who showed me that the best way of provoking honesty in the thought processes and in the behavior of others is to practice it.

. . .

It is absurd that even now I am diffident about expressing my feelings to you. . . . But the reserve of real life dogs me. . . . Shall I take the plunge? — and say that I loved you.

IV. Becoming an "Educated Man"

Early Acquaintances at Harvard — Choral Music — Piano Lessons — History and English — "Fine Ahts" — Philosophy — Touring with the Double Quartet — Camp Wigwam — The Liberal Club — From Langdon Warner to Irving Babbitt — Decision for the Harpsichord — Performances and a Fellowship — Other Musical Activities — The "Educated Man"

It is hard for me to believe that the development of the next six years took place in so short a time. I blossomed like desert vegetation on which rain has begun to fall. From North Leominster to Cambridge I had gone but a short distance eastward toward a Promised Land, continuing the trend of my parents that had reversed the westward drive of my pioneer ancestors. But five years later, still further eastward and still further back into the past, I was to find in Europe a second Promised Land. The progress in six years from *Aufschwung* in the Leominster City Hall to an admiring reception in Berlin and Salzburg was more than either my mother or I could have possibly foreseen.

Harvard was already a university and one was free to roam among the most diverse kinds of interests and people. There was little of the social pressure that still dominated most smaller American colleges. My liberation was complete. I was surrounded by fascinating characters and first-rate minds.

Many of my first friendships were made either in the dining halls, where I waited on table in order to supplement the thousand dollars a year which my father had promised me, or around the piano when I played in the Common Rooms. But perhaps the most far-reaching of my early contacts was that with William Aydelotte, the son of the then president of Swarthmore College, and with his roommate Frank Lowell, a distant cousin of the president of Harvard. The contrast between the two could hardly have been greater. Bill Aydelotte, peering near-sightedly through thick glasses, enormous and ill-coordinated, qualified as one of Harvard's best eccentrics, whereas

Frank Lowell looked like a blond Apollo newly descended from the skies. To them I owe my first glimpses of a kind of life both elegant and rich in spiritual resources of which I had not previously dreamed, much less experienced.

The Lowell household in Concord, to which I was invited before long, became for me (but I think infinitely more stimulating) what that of the Guermantes was to the narrator in Proust. Guests of all ages were continually coming and going, and in that house I first encountered characters as diverse as Samuel Eliot Morison and Lincoln Kirstein.

A more exotic household, by any standards, was that of Bill Aydelotte's cousin, Mrs. Fiske Warren. The blinds of her house on Beacon Hill were always drawn, and the woodwork of hallway, parlors and dining room painted in dull black. From the walls came a dim glow of silver Chinese tea-chest paper, and what light there was fell upon innumerable hanging balls of colored glass and on the gold initials of a wrinkled choirbook that lay open in the back parlor. Peering through its darkness, one advanced with hushed footfalls toward the fireplace, to be greeted from behind a teatray by a lady of indeterminate age (in fact, I cannot recall ever seeing her in broad daylight), who talked in reverent sybilline tones of Meister Eckhart, John Donne and many other things that we did not fully understand. Never was her husband in evidence. I am told that she is believed to have inspired certain elements in T.S. Eliot's "Portrait of a Lady." She appears to have held generation after generation of Harvard students spellbound and mystified. Her likeness by Sargent hung over the mantel of the front parlor, but it was not one of Sargent's best. She was perhaps too unworldly for that most urbane of painters, and her portrait rather resembled a dead fish.

For Harvard undergraduates the most conspicuous member of the Music Department was Archibald T. Davison, "Doc," as generations of Harvard men always called him. He was one of the first in this country to divert a university glee club to the singing of classical music and to raise its performances to a level that made it together with the Radcliffe Choral Society the chief source of choral parts for major works played by the Boston Symphony. He was profoundly musical, even if the style of his performances would not always meet with the approval of the knowledgeable of today, and he had a charisma that could inspire boundless devotion and enthusiasm. Why I did not immediately join the Glee Club I can no longer recall; perhaps it was because I had never yet myself sung anything but hymns and school songs, both of which I hated. In my sophomore year I was an unsuccessful candidate for a post as one of the accompanists for the Glee Club. This failure disappointed me greatly, and I did not realize until much later how fortunate it was that I had the experience of singing rather than playing. Although my voice was never good, choral singing did more to train my ear and musical perceptions than all my studies at the keyboard.

At Harvard I found a number of pianists who played far better than I, and that my rhythmic instabilities (which doubtless caused my rejection as Glee Club accompanist) were painfully evident when ensemble playing was attempted. At any rate, instrumental resources were not very great at Harvard in my time, and there were never more than one or two cellists available in the entire university. (The same was still true at Yale in 1940 when Paul Hindemith and I first joined the music faculty!) A trio formed with colleagues from my first-year harmony class and beginning with the Mendelssohn E minor soon came to shipwreck on insurmountable difficulties of the other two pieces that I had picked out, the César Franck in F sharp minor and the Ravel.

Not long after I had made the acquaintance of the Lowell family, Mrs. Lowell arranged that I should go to see Thomas Whitney Surette and play for him. Mr. Surette had been a partner of Doc Davison in their joint effort to raise the level of music as sung in churches and taught in schools. Because I had heard he liked Bach, I decided to play the Italian Concerto. I had never heard anyone else play it, nor had I ever heard any other Bach concerto, nor indeed a concerto of any kind. But I had the idea that piano concertos were free exhibitions of the player's capriciousness and fantasy, and I did my best to render the Italian Concerto the vehicle chiefly of my own rhythmic freedom. Mr. Surette said little, but in his crusty New England way suggested that I needed further teaching and offered to procure me a scholarship with Mr. Wesley Weyman, who taught for a day or two a week in Boston. I learned afterwards that Mr.

50

Surette had told Mrs. Lowell that while I played atrociously he thought I was bursting with talent.

Mr. Weyman was a man of some culture, neither a particularly good pianist nor a profound musician, but he had much to give that I badly needed. Like his predecessors and like my poor mother, he had a hard time getting me to understand the need for discipline. He straightened out some of my worst eccentricities and directed me toward a greater sobriety of style.

My official studies seem to have formed only a small part of my new and exciting existence. Apart from first-year harmony, I can remember only two of the courses I took. European History, as administered by Roger Merriman (Frisky), with rich and abundant reading assignments, was a superb course to which thousands of Harvard freshmen were compulsorily exposed both before and after my time. At sixteen I was not yet ready for all its benefits, and I absorbed much less than I would have later. Frisky had academic *panache*; in addition to being a good scholar and impressive lecturer he could freeze any latecomer with a glint of his one glass eye or bellow to some hapless person whose manners were unacceptable, "Take off your hat, Sir!"

The required course in English composition was taught in my section by Fredson Bowers, later a well-known bibliographer. It was responsible, among other productions, for my complete poetical works, early, middle, and late. These consisted of a few laboriously fabricated sonnets produced with much counting of syllables on fingers. Harvard has – or had – a laudable custom of retaining the compositions of its freshmen and returning them on request only at graduation, in the hope that the student may be aware of his own improvement after four years. I never bothered to recover mine, but I find that I must have kept most of the rough drafts. They are not masterpieces.

Independently of the assignments in English composition, I kept for a brief time a kind of journal into which I made sporadic entries. I have found one dated January 28, 1928, which more that fifty years beforehand admirably prophesied some of the difficulties which I continue to have.

My expression is abominable and very unsuccessful. When I rake over my experiences and thoughts systematically I become boring and rather silly. And if I resort to the sketchy style of my letters, setting down what first comes into my head, the journal degenerates into a mere diary, an amplification of line a day. . . . But there seems to be a want for expression in some way. . . . Perhaps greater success would or will come with maturity.

I continued on February 19, 1928:

I am getting a much deeper understanding of the art of poetry from my recent attempts. Apparently, one not a master craftsman nor with a greatly gifted mind, must sit and court fickle inspiration. Another disconcerting, if not ludicrous thing is the way in which poets' ideas manage to form themselves to fit the verse-form properly, with the aim still to preserve the appearance of sincerity and original intention. . . .

How futile it is to make statements about poetry, which is always as intangible as art or beauty. I have found that one does not write intellectual poetry. Reasoning is too tangible; something much more subtle is necessary to vivify good poetry.

The horizons opened up during my first year at Harvard had so broadened my interests that my notions had changed concerning the direction of official studies. I realized that without "concentrating" in music I could get out of the music department all I wanted and yet avoid certain courses that were generally considered a waste of time. Since my interests were primarily esthetic I disposed of the required "distribution" in science by taking a general course in biology in my junior year and letting my classmates perform most of the laboratory work for me. I felt no need for further study in English literature, other than to find the time to sit down alone with the books themselves. I had no wish to sit at the feet of famous prima donnas like Kittredge and Lowes, or to study Latin or Greek classics, nor was I tempted by the historians.

In visual matters, although I had always paid a certain amount of attention to architecture, my taste and knowledge had never developed much beyond the decorative arts. Sensing the need to develop further acquaintance and sensibility, I decided to fix my official "concentration" on what in the prevailing Boston accent was known as "Fine Ahts." Although I was ultimately exposed to a lot of art-historical claptrap, my musical development lost absolutely nothing by this decision, and my subsequent years, especially those in Europe, were thereby rendered infinitely richer.

I began with courses in classical and western European art and learned to identify and comment on vast quantities of photographs and slides, using much the same processes of memory that have always made it easy for me to retain the titles of books and the spellings of words, and I soon learned to manipulate the jargon of art history. Like many of the others who have taken and are still taking degrees in "Fineahts" at Harvard, I had not the faintest glimmer of any talent for drawing, painting or design. Therefore the course which caused me the greatest agony was Arthur Pope's introductory course, in which we were required to manipulate watercolors to illustrate his terminology of color values, to paint a still life or two, to draw from frescoes of Giotto and plaster casts of Michelangelo, and to copy prints and drawings in various media of artists ranging from Haranobu to Rembrandt and Turner. This course, its equivalent now unpardonably suppressed (since art historians like musicologists apparently manipulate words or jargon most freely when uninhibited by any first-hand knowledge of what they are talking about), did more to sharpen my visual perceptions than almost any other experience of my life. To think that at the time we were so bored by it!

Another very good course which however I took while still too young fully to profit by it was a survey of western European philosophy led by Ralph Barton Perry, who had made his studies at Harvard in the time of Santayana, James and Royce. Much attention was paid to Plato and Aristotle. Plato appealed to me and I have often returned to him, despite his failure in my view to understand the arts any better than many a present-day academic. Aristotle appealed to me not at all, and there is much in his influence on subsequent artistic theory that I have always found unacceptable. We read Epictetus, Marcus Aurelius and Lucretius. As I recall, the Middle Ages were passed over rather lightly in the year in which I took the course, and we then took up Bacon and Descartes.

To Descartes I have often returned; in fact I count him as one of my spiritual ancestors. Yet only recently have I been made able to surmount the absurdities of his physiology by the suggestion of my friend the engraver Roger Vieillard, who illustrated the *Discours de la Méthode*, that it is best read as a kind of poem.

We read considerable stretches of Spinoza's *Ethics*, but I cannot recall its influencing me. Visiting professors were frequently called into the course and I heard two or three lectures by the prestigious Alfred North Whitehead without understanding a word of what he was talking about. We read Hume and Kant; or rather I was supposed to have read Kant, but my extracurricular musical activities had me so fully occupied and away from Cambridge at the time of the relevant lectures that I was obliged to bluff outrageously in the final examination. By way of expiation I have had a German edition of his complete works on my shelves for the last forty years but have not opened them more than once or twice! Schopenhauer however got my full attention, and I was delighted by the use made in his esthetic theories of notions resembling the Platonic Ideas, and by his criticism of Haydn for trying to represent Chaos in the *Creation* in contradiction to the fact that music by its very nature can only be considered as a form of Order.

I was now singing in the Glee Club and the Bach Cantata Club, accompanying a classmate in German *Lieder*, performing new compositions by Harvard friends, and on January 30, 1929 I made my operatic debut in the Boston Opera House with the Chicago Opera Company (silent, fortunately) as an Egyptian slave in *Aïda*. But my major musical commitment involved accompanying an organization called the University Double Quartet, a pocketsized imitation of the Harvard Glee Club and its repertoire. In addition to the vocal ensemble pieces, I accompanied its director, Douglas MacKinnon, in *Lieder* and played a group of piano solos. My principal warhorses appear to have been piano pieces of Brahms, most particularly Opus 119. In two motor cars we toured the east of the United States as far south as Washington and as far west as Buffalo, to the extent of giving approximately forty concerts a season in prep schools and colleges. I was paid a badly needed ten dollars a concert.

Tours were arranged as far as possible to coincide with Harvard vacations, but every so often I was obliged to miss a week or two of classes and of the work relevant to them. This I compensated by perfecting that part of a college education which is most useful in later life, namely by learning how to create a good impression out of absolutely nothing, learning in examinations to use words to imply knowledge I did not possess and convincingly to discuss reading I had never done.

I find a letter written to my family in the midst of that tour of 1928 which must have been responsible for my lasting ignorance of the works of Immanuel Kant. I had just been in New York for the first time, and after a long account of the sights most frequented by newcomers, and of the Metropolitan Museum, where even then I found the pictures "so badly hung," I ended up with the exclamation, "I am perfectly crazy about New York." This was a sentiment not destined to endure. I declared also that "Both Yale and Princeton are much more beautiful than Harvard."

The pianos I encountered ranged in quality from the inspiring to the outrageous, and many times in later years, when struggling with a particularly recalcitrant harpsichord, I could recall that pianists have no such easy time of it either! After the next two years of touring with the Double Quartet and of facing the exasperating, bizarre and comic adventures which it presented, I was a hardened trouper, and came to touring in later life not fully unprepared.

Through Mr. Surette I obtained a job for the summer of 1929 as a music counselor in a Jewish boys camp, Camp Wigwam, in Harrison, Maine. Summer camps in those days employed as counselors a curious mixture of college students, teachers supplementing their incomes, artists whose careers insufficiently supported them, and a certain proportion of out-and-out misfits, derelicts and has-beens. The level at Wigwam was fairly high, and since one of its directors loved music and was a celebrity chaser, we had a number of distinguished visitors, among them Leopold Godowsky, for whom I turned pages as he played some of his most complicated and note-laden transcriptions on a little upright Steinway sent in for the occasion. My principal function turned out to be the coaching and accompanying of a production of *The Pirates of Penzance*, an occupation which forever cured me of any previous ability to put up with anything whatever by Gilbert and Sullivan. I returned to Cambridge ready to kiss its dirtiest sidewalk.

In September of 1929 Wesley Weyman rendered me his greatest service. For some reason or other we met in the Harvard Yard, and as we walked up and down, he announced the termination of my lessons with him and gave me such a dressing-down as I have never had before or since. It concerned my irresponsibility, my lack of discipline, my disregard for other people, and many other defects of my character the long enumeration of which I have forgotten, but it was devastating. The timing was right. He stripped me of every vestige of self-esteem, and for months I felt that there was no health in me. I saw my only salvation in discipline and sustained concentrated effort. He had accomplished what my mother and previous well-wishers had vainly tried to do. Whether Mr. Weyman's timing and terminology were deliberate, I have never known. Once or twice in desperation but with a cool head I have tried this kind of shock-treatment on pupils of mine, but without such success.

From this moment my conscience left me no possibility of remaining a dilettante, except in those areas in which I had never had any pretense of seriousness. In terms of musical and intellectual responsibility, my work was now cut out for me, and I struggled frantically to regain some right to self-respect. It was not at all unfortunate for me that at this same time I was forced into full financial responsibility for my maintenance and for my future. My father, who had promised me a thousand dollars a year for the duration of my undergraduate studies, had retired unexpectedly early, and well before the Crash of 1929 had suffered such reverses in his investments as wiped out much of what he had counted on for his later years, so that after my first two years he found himself obliged to withdraw his promise. From my eighteenth birthday onward, I never again received a penny from home. I not only had to earn money but I had also to make sure that my academic work would be of a quality sufficient to assure me support from scholarships.

How I met my financial emergencies I no longer recall, except that I resumed waiting on table, a practice I had given up the previous year, and that I added the paid function of bass in the University Choir to my other extracurricular activities. Most of the course work of this year has sunk into oblivion or insignificance, but it was in this year that I took a course in the history of print-making with Paul

Sachs. Working directly with the catalogues and collections of the Fogg Print Room, I became familiar with the major works of European print-makers and formed my first preferences for works that years later I was able to add to my own collection. Mr. Sachs used a method for focussing our attention that I have never forgotten. He would throw on a screen a slide for example, of a wood-cut or an engraving by Dürer, and ask us to note on paper everything, but really everything that we could bring ourselves to see in it. For this deceptively simple method of setting in motion and sharpening the visual perceptions I owe a lifetime of gratitude. Paul Sachs was one of that nearly extinct race of connoisseurs who regarded works of art as materials of experience and not as mere objects for study.

In October or November of 1929 I was first ushered into the presence of a harpsichord that had recently been given to Harvard. I have spoken of it elsewhere, but I have not mentioned that the first sounds I heard coming from it were not those of Bach or Scarlatti, but rather of jazz played on it by one of the instructors in the Music Department. I later obtained further access to this instrument, and amid much experimenting learned some pieces which I played in May 1930 at a public concert of the Harvard Music Club. I was still quite unaware that this event was so heavy with consequences, more than forty years of them!

During the years of my exposure to Brahms through choral singing and through performances of the Boston Symphony my admiration and enthusiasm grew to a point from which, alas, it could only decline ever since. I now have that gingerly relation with his music that one has with an outlived lover or former spouse, when an encounter brings a saddening reminder of vanished former joys and only rarely an indication that something in the relationship remains intact. My allegiance however has never wavered to certain works like the Alto Rhapsody and the B flat Piano Concerto. In 1930 the announcement of a Brahms Festival in Symphony Hall brought me to the highest pitch of excitement and anticipation. We of the Glee Club were to participate in the Requiem, the *Schicksalslied*, the Alto Rhapsody (with Matzenauer) and I was admitted to the special group that performed the *Liebeslieder*. All the symphonies and various other orchestra pieces were included in the plans and Arthur Schnabel was invited to play both concertos and some piano pieces. For years after his performance of the B flat Concerto I never cared to hear anyone else play it. After that concert and the Fourth Symphony which its program also included, I remember walking home along the Charles in a mystical state of ecstasy which I cannot explain, but which still overtakes me when I hear the opening measures of the Concerto. Had anyone then suggested to me that I would one day prefer the *Années de Pèlerinage* of Liszt to all the piano pieces of Brahms, I would have flung him into the river.

For the summer of 1930 Mr. Surette had procured me another job at a camp, this time a girls camp, Ogontz in Lisbon, New Hampshire. I was made much happier there than at Wigwam by not being obliged to live in a tent with six or eight little boys. There was the usual staff of counselors with its customary supplement of misfits and derelicts. I played for assemblies, for dance classes, coached a chorus and supplied music for a rather odd set of Sunday morning services presided over by the headmistress of the camp. These were neo-pantheistic in character, with much mixing up of the natural and the divine, and took place, weather permitting, in a pine grove at the top of a hill. On a set of tubular chimes I hammered out hymn tunes and bits of plainchant, and once we got the harmonium fixed (the squirrels had eaten up its bellows), I played on it such Bach preludes as the slow-speaking action of an old-fashioned harmonium could be expected to deliver.

It was at Ogontz in the following summer that I bade an unlamented farewell to the dramatic stage. It seemed at the time that every female teacher of French in the United States cherished an ambition one day to play Rostand's *L'Aiglon*, generally following as closely as possible the manner of the late Sarah Bernhardt. To this rule Mme. Malécot at Ogontz was no exception, and a performance was announced for the end of the summer. My services were enlisted for the role of Metternich. Needless to say, the play was very much reduced, and I have forgotten what the other roles were. But fortunately mine was cut to the bone in favor of Mme. Malécot's Aiglon in white riding breeches. I don't know why, but I think I wore riding boots too, and shifting stiffly from attitude to attitude, declaimed my hexameters in sonorous Massachusetts French.

In the fall of 1930 the first two installments of the new Harvard House Plan went into effect, and I became the first occupant of a brand-new suite of rooms in Lowell House. By some miracle — it may have been an augmented scholarship — I was able to give up waiting on table and subsequently the Double Quartet, to the great benefit of my academic work and my social life. I remained in the Choir and other singing organizations, assumed the musical direction of the King's Chapel Sunday School in Boston, and further augmented my income by giving a few piano lessons.

By now I had learned how to plan my work, to organize the hierarchy of essentials and subsidiaries, to submit to the discipline of one plodding methodical step after another in order to accomplish a desired purpose, but I had also learned when absolutely necessary to improvise and bluff my way through. When I consider the array of courses in which I was involved during the academic year of 1930–31, I am surprised that I was able to do aceptable work in any of them. But it appears that one way or another I passed them all with honors, that is, all but beginning German, although two years later I was to do my first teaching and lecturing in that language. In Fine Arts I was doing a course in North Italian painting that so familiarized me with all important paintings and their locations that a year later when in Verona, Padua, Venice and Milan for the first time I hardly needed a guidebook to direct me to any of the many pictures I wished to see. I was also working with Langdon Warner in Chinese and Japanese art and preparing for my general examinations in the history of some five thousand years of Western art.

As an exception to my usual rule of avoiding literature courses because of my preference for doing the reading for myself, I took Irving Babbitt's course in the Romantic Movement. Irving Babbitt in the promulgation of his New Humanism was one of the most influential members of the Harvard faculty. Loaded down with literature he would assume his place at the lecturer's desk, and piling books on either side of him while managing to flip the pages of two books at the same time, one in each hand, in a flat Indiana accent he undertook his demolition of the thought of Shelley and Wordsworth. His presentation was anything but objective — and infinitely stimulating. One after the other he would sweep away those romantic cobwebs which then obscured our vision more seriously than now, for the Second World War has performed the same work in infinitely more devastating fashion. My innate dislike of Rousseau found welcome reinforcement at his hands. Babbitt was more interested in ideas than in poetry, and he was very hard on some justly vulnerable but very good poetry. Wordsworth's *Intimations of Immortality* and Keats's *Grecian Urn*, not to mention the *Nightingale*, were among his special targets. He never tired of taking potshots at Primitivism, Man's Inherent Goodness, Progress, Sensibility, and at the disasters latent in Goethe's attitude toward the second part of *Faust*, anything that with a snarl he could label as "Denial of Dualism." I wrote a wretched paper on the German Lied and its texts, but Harry Levin, who was a mere sophomore at the time, produced a paper that won a prize and was immediately published as the first item in a long bibliography that extends through his present tenure as Irving Babbitt Professor.

In music I was taking the only courses that might be called music history to which I have ever been subjected in my entire life, "Doc" Davison's course in the history of choral music, and as sole student a special project on the history of harpsichord music, about which at the time he knew as little as I. My remaining music course, Wallace Woodworth's in the music of Bach, was an innovation that year, and I had already been asked to perform the harpsichord and clavichord illustrations for it. This brought about my preparing to perform, among other works, the Goldberg Variations for what is probably the first time they had been played on the harpsichord anywhere in the United States, even in a room as small as our classroom in Paine Hall. At that time they were commonly regarded as unpalatable and unsuitable for performance. This enterprise occupied a great deal of my time and ambition. In addition, I had been asked to play the Bach D minor Concerto with the University Orchestra.

Already in December 1930 it had dawned on me that of all the things I felt capable of doing, engaging in the cultivation of early keyboard music, especially that of Bach on the harpsichord and clavichord, was the one that most needed to be done. Although I had no expectation whatever of a concert career such as ultimately

60

developed, I intended to focus all my activities around this undertaking, whatever they might have to be.

By the time I had entered Harvard I knew that despite my many other interests music would be my profession, and that I would need further study after graduating. Now, at the height of the Depression, how and where would it be possible; how to avoid being thrust into an unwanted and irrelevant job merely for the sake of earning money? I was again at a crossroads, as before the decision to come to Harvard. The remainder of my life might have been quite, quite different!

The performance of the Goldberg Variations and of the other works for the Bach class was creditable, I think, perhaps remarkable in view of my inexperience. The public performance of the Concerto went well and attracted the favorable attention of the crustiest writer on music of the Boston press. In any case, my fate was decided on March 13, when the Music Department, overlooking the fact that I was a concentrator in Fine Arts and not in Music, nevertheless awarded me a Paine Travelling Fellowship for study in Europe.

The remainder of the spring brought a rush of musical events, term papers, and cramming for examinations. At the Bach Festival of the Boston Symphony in March, the B minor Mass was performed in Boston for the first time since 1901 [I think], and for the first long-anticipated time I could hear it complete. It was however the last time that I sang in it, and later performances when I played continuo on the harpsichord were disappointing — they never carried me away by involving every fiber of my body as completely as this one in which I sang. There are advantages in having to wait four years in eager anticipation to hear a work that nowadays can be casually overheard coming through a loudspeaker at a cocktail party.

In April the Glee Club sang in Town Hall in New York (my first participation in a concert there) and at the Metropolitan Opera (my first and last appearance on that stage) in a performance of Stravinsky's *Oedipus Rex* under Leopold Stowkowski. We had rehearsed it all winter. (A few years ago it was done in a good performance at Yale with less than a week's rehearsal for all concerned, so familiar has its musical language now become.)

61

Back in Cambridge I had a chronological and geographical chart of Western art since ancient Egypt tacked up in my bathroom for easier memorization of dates and names in preparation for my general examinations. George Kirstein and I sat up all of one or more nights cramming for the finals in Babbitt's course; in fact I hardly ever slept. Other friends helped me copy musical examples for my term papers on Bach and on harpsichord music, and went around impressing other non-musicians by talking learnedly of Froberger and Frescobaldi. I was preparing a small harpsichord recital for the end of June for the Surette School (actually the program was hardly small; it was endless!). And everyone was giving me advice on what to do the following year in Europe.

At Commencement in Sever Quadrangle, when President Lowell had finished conferring our degrees he welcomed us "to the Fellowship of Educated Men." We were all terrible snobs, but some of us looked questioningly at one another. To this day I cannot believe that he meant literally what he said. Many of us had sense enough to know that we still had nearly everything to learn, although not all of us were sure that we knew quite what. I at least knew that much of the entire craft of music remained for me to master, that despite what I had learned about music, my technical skills had remained largely undeveloped through my four undergraduate years. I had merely found out how to discipline and to make use of what I already had. The verbalism of academic education had threatened to make me confuse knowledgeability with experience. Never have I entirely divested myself of a certain self-satisfied intellectual snobbery, but in the years since Harvard many inroads have been made upon it. It was fortunate for me that my physical instincts were very strong, and that I tend to believe and remember only that which I can apprehend through the senses and through action based on sensory impressions. Nevertheless, the Word with me has constantly risked being valued as highly, or more highly, than the Deed.

At some moment I had the good idea of pasting into a scrapbook the question sheets of the examinations to which I submitted while at Harvard. The collection is not entirely complete, but the grades that I marked on them seem to indicate that I passed them all. My head swims at the notion of trying to pass any of them now. Only to a few relatively simple questions have I ready answers. It is of course true that by cramming all night and by resorting to my old techniques of bluffing, my accumulated experience might permit me to do even better than forty-odd years ago.

But a comparable dizziness overtakes me when I survey the titles of those term papers that I have kept but not re-read. They deal with such diverse subjects as *The Upper Classes in England at About 1708–1718; Gardens in Ancient Egypt; The Development of Mantegna's Emotional Attitude Toward His Art; The Material Culture of the Han Dynasty*; and, more understandably *The Interpretation of the Keyboard Music of Bach*. Perhaps, after all, President Lowell was alluding to the old saying that an educated man is one who has forgotten more than other people have ever learned. But humility never was, nor is a common virtue at Harvard.

Part Two

EUROPEAN JOURNAL: 1931–1933

In September 1931, my departure for Europe once again continued my reversal of the westward-bound search of my ancestors for the future Promised Land. My Promised Land lay eastward, and in large measure in a past that I was eager to rediscover. My immediate goal was Paris. My principal aims were the recovery of harpsichord and clavichord techniques and of a command of the musical literature and source material relating to the performance of solo and chamber music. My practical goal was harpsichord study with Wanda Landowska, research in the Bibliothèque Nationale, and the filling of many gaps in my basic musicianship through study with Nadia Boulanger.

On the boat crossing the Atlantic I began a letter-journal which gives a more complete and vivid account of the next two years than I could possibly give today. In the excerpts that follow, I have made no changes except to normalize punctuation and capitalization, and to correct a few errors in spelling. All excisions within sentences are indicated by the usual three dots. I have suppressed many passages dealing with the visual arts and with the usual objects of tourist attention. They contain too much that is second-hand, jargon carried over from my art-historical studies at Harvard, and they concern themselves with objects and scenes that have been frequently and better described. On the whole, however, I feel that a large portion of what I wrote about music rings true. It can stand as a genuine expression of my feelings and opinions at the time.

| | Somewhere in the middle |
| Wednesday, September 23, 1931 | of the Atlantic |

We pulled out of Brooklyn last night about 12:30 in a surreptitious and most unsensational way. So far the ocean has been very smooth and the sun has been shining. But it is clouding up. All this morning, after a rather bad night's sleep in a stuffy cabin, I dozed deliciously under the sun in a streamer chair. The third class quarters here are all at the forward end of the ship, so that it is hard to realize how really long the boat is. We have a comfortable modernistic salon and smoking room. Practically everyone is German, and I quite enjoy using my small supply of the language.

September 26

The sky cleared this afternoon and the wind abated. At sundown the sky and sea were beautiful with glowing clouds piled high around the horizon, and the waves and foam washing silver in the light. I find it very difficult to imagine the vast expanse that lies beyond the limited horizon, and the conception of landing in France, day after tomorrow is quite impossible.

Tuesday morning, September 29   Paris! Hôtel du Quai Voltaire

Here I am, still somewhat bewildered but fascinated with the city. Here I am sitting in a red plush chair in front of a long French window with a little wrought-iron balcony, facing directly on the Quai Voltaire and the Seine, with the Louvre on the opposite bank of the river. The walls of the sidewalks next to the river are lined with little booksellers' stands, which are now just being opened up.

After changing my clothes and first buying a map of Paris, I walked out across the bridge to the Louvre into the old quadrangle. One has to become accustomed to the patchy dirtiness of all French buildings including Notre Dame. The soot settles only in certain places leaving projections white against the black. Then I walked down past the Palais de Justice to Notre Dame.

Being then very hungry I went into a restaurant and had a somewhat patchy dinner, partly because of a quite illegible French menu, but it was very good. By the time I got to the Pont Neuf, I was so sleeply I was sure I would fall asleep in the middle of the street and be annihilated by one of the dreadful French taxicabs. (They all call each other names, and have the most awful fights with pedestrians.) My taxidriver yesterday had about three encounters to each block. He nearly ran over one irate man with a long brown beard, who shook his cane at him and called him a "cochon vert" (green pig).

There is a little oval basin on a stand here, about the size of a small baby's bath — I don't know whether I dare take a sponge bath in it or not! One other thing to do today: find out how the French take baths.

October 4, 1931   21 Rue Jacob, Paris
I have at last found a room and am established in it, on the cinquième (really sixth floor) in a pension where I get all my meals. The Rue Jacob is on the left bank, in the old quarter, not far from the river opposite the old part of the Louvre. Every quarter hour I hear the bells of St.-Germain-des-Prés, the oldest church in Paris. The house has a paved courtyard, and in back is a charming little garden with trees and bits of antique sculpture in grey stone. A spiral staircase, slippery with wax, leads up to my room, which is quite large, with a floor of old red octagonal titles (alas, a dreadful red carpet), a nice fireplace, and a large casement window looking on the court, and a tiny window up beside the head of my bed from which I can just see the tops of the towers of St. Sulpice.

Paris is really a marvelous city, succeeding with perfect grace and charming atmosphere in all these elements that make other cities so depressing, grand boulevards and parkways, monumental buildings decorated with all kinds of sculptural garbage, slums, dirt, smells, fashionable shops. The Seine is the nicest river in the world, and equally dirty! Paris traffic is completely crazy. Cars never stay on the right side of the street, and as soon as you step off the curb, come shooting at you from all directions. The only traffic regulation seems to be the survival of the biggest and heaviest car and the toughest and most resilient pedestrian. They have policemen who stand at every intersection and wave billy-clubs and egg on the furious battle of taxi drivers. No one ever minds the policeman, nor does the policeman seem to expect anyone to stop when he tells them to.

October 13, 1931
Wednesday I again found Mlle. Boulanger not returned to the city.

Thursday afternoon I took the train out to St. Leu la Forêt to see Landowska. While she was engaged with lessons, her secretary took me around and introduced me to some of the hocus pocus and some of the pupils. "Yes," she said, "Wanda Landowska is a truly wonderful person. She can do anything. Yes, she even planned this garden. You've heard about the concert hall. We call it the Temple, devoted to old music," etc.

"Holy jumping cats," I thought, "what am I getting into." My amazement increased when we entered the hall and found a perfect negro mammy, Landowska's chief pupil in costume having his picture taken. There were a number of women, one the kind that gives you a finger instead of a whole hand, and a number of old harpsichords obviously chosen for decorative rather than musical effect, in a very nice room with two Pleyel harpsichords and two Pleyel pianos ensconced on a little raised platform. I was somewhat alarmed by the hocus pocusness of the atmosphere and the general spirit of "Isn't this old music just lovely. And nobody can play it but Landowska!"

Some time later came a hush, and Landowska entered. She is a sort of combination of Mrs. Landowsky, the pawn broker's wife, and Wanda, daughter of Henry VIII, sister of Mary and Elizabeth. I shook her hand, which she withdrew quickly, and said, "Oh, be careful. My harpsichord hand!" However, she was very nice in a sort of come-into-the-parlor-Red-Riding-Hood way.

Then she and pupils rehearsed some music for two harpsichords, and as she was very tired, and as I was a bit swamped in hocus pocus, I was not much pleased with her playing, which seemed rather dry, resembling nothing so much as a well-bred typewriter, rather than a well-tempered clavichord. I found her registration quite contrary to the structure of the music, and her phrasing the exact opposite of anything I had found out about Bach's phrasing. I began to wonder what I was going to do.

I became acquainted with one of the pupils, a very nice American woman, who had much sound information and advice. I decided to attend the classes, at least, till I saw what Wanda had to give, then possibly take private lessons. The enclosed price list will explain some of my qualms, as I wished to see more of Landowska than her virtuosity at raking in the shekels.

I went back on Saturday to her class, which was really simply more rehearsing of music for two harpsichords, violin, and voice also. There I was considerably more favorably impressed, particularly with the rhythmic precision and clarity of her technic and her specifically harpsichord touch, and I realized what much needed benefit I would derive from a thorough grounding of technic, although I did not approve of many details, and although one must question her interpretations constantly for historical accuracy and stylistic consistency. She made me play for her and told me that I was very talented and had a good hand, but needed technic.

That same evening I met a German woman who was studying with Landowska, a pupil of Ramin, the Leipzig man. She said that Ramin was a great man and musician, but not particularly accurate historically, and not even attempting to teach much technic. He told her that he learned most of his own technic from watching Landowska play. She advised getting a thorough technical grounding before going to Ramin. This information, although surprising, was somewhat reassuring. After all, Landowska has played the harpsichord longer than anyone else.

My further capitulation came on Sunday, when this same music was given a dress rehearsal, plus some solo playing by Landowska, and the Mozart sonata for two pianos, played by Landowska and Gerlin, her chief pupil. And really, — I have only once heard Mozart playing that even approached the precision, brilliance, and delicacy of hers, and the way she could turn and mold the phrases and simply take you straight to heaven in the slow movements. Her piano tone is always the same color, although with variations, ranging toward hardness, but it makes little difference. And her harpsichord registration is often very effective, as well as her playing, although frequently unsound stylistically. She is a much greater musician than I first thought her.

This afternoon I went down to Pleyel's with Gerlin and picked out a fairly good upright piano to rent. I was sorely tempted by a perfect Bechstein grand, but decided it to be an extravagance. Then I took a lesson with Gerlin. He is giving me the preliminary exercises before

I start taking private lessons with Landowska. The exercises are based upon an old-fashioned system of technic quite different from the kind of piano-playing I have most recently learned, and have a tendency to make me stiff. Also I must guard against the bad tone characteristic of both Gerlin's and Landowska's playing. But they will be very good for me.

P.S. It might be a good thing to preserve these letters, as they form a fairly complete record.

Tuesday, October 20, 1931

I went to the first counterpoint class of Mlle. Boulanger, who was quite different from my expectations. In general appearance, particularly dress, she looks like the geometry teacher in a middle west high school, except for evidence of a tremendously keen and sensitive intelligence. She is obviously a born teacher, with a tremendous interest in her pupils and almost any phase of teaching. I liked very much the way she conducted the class. I am very thankful that she is such a contrast to Landowska, whom I do not like personally.

In the evening I went out to St. Denis for the concert of Landowska and her pupils, given in a local movie theatre, a perfect barn of a place, and was pressed into service as a page turner, faded blue suit and all. I had hoped to see something of the cathedral, but in the dark I saw only the rather squat-looking exterior. I shall make another expedition sometime.

I went out to Landowska's to tea. She had read my papers on Bach and harpsichord music, and wanted me to do some research work under her supervision, and spoke of publication of works of her pupils in a "St. Leu series." My apprehension that it would be a project better avoided was later confirmed by Mrs. Curzon,* the most interesting and intelligent of her pupils.

I had a session with Mrs. Curzon at the harpsichord at the Salle Pleyel, in which we compared notes and played for each other. She has been very helpful in introducing me to the intricacies of dealing

---

* The American harpsichordist Lucille Wallace (d. 1977), wife of the noted pianist Clifford Curzon (1907–1982).

with Landowska. Now that she has returned to England, I shall very much miss someone with whom I can safely discuss such problems. This afternoon I went out to St. Leu for one of Landowska's classes. She gave me some more exercises, perfectly terrific ones. I think she is probably wasting a good deal of my time, but the residuum of gain, particularly in precision and strength, will be worthwhile. I rather dread working on interpretation, because in a good many ways I shall never wish to imitate her, and there is no question of discussion with her. One simply swallows everything without question and regurgitates privately. She wants to keep almost complete control over her pupils in almost every field of activity, in a most useless way. This afternoon I asked her if I could read her copy of the rare "L'Art de Toucher le Clavecin" of Couperin and she said, "Yes, we will go over it paragraph by paragraph." I shall read it at the Bibliothèque Nationale!

Tuesday, October 27, 1931

In the evening, Hubert [Lamb] * and I went for a walk and indulged in a rather lame philosophical speculation in the court of the Louvre, beginning by wondering when and how the Louvre and Notre Dame would lie in ruins, stone quarries for the peasants.

November 2, 1931

Friday afternoon I had a lesson with Mlle. Boulanger, and worked in the library of the Conservatoire. Mlle. Boulanger is a most remarkable person, of the greatest insight and sensibility. She could probably teach the very stones.

I went out to St. Leu for the course, but Landowska being ill, I practiced the harpsichord all afternoon. I worked out a fingering and a very nice registration for one of the Little Preludes of Bach, which I shall have the temerity to show Landowska, who will probably tear it to pieces. It seemed good to approach real music. I am practically sure that after I have acquired Landowska's technic, I can develop resources of the harpsichord, which she and particularly her pupils

---

* Hubert Lamb (Harvard, 1930, and a Paine Fellow) and his wife Lydia were — and remained — close friends of RK.

71

have not touched, particularly in the way of tone production. There was a great deal of advantage in taking up the harpsichord by myself, because by experiment I found out a lot of things that I might have ignored had I a teacher to rely on. Most of Landowska's pupils are a dreadful bunch of dilettante girls (the men are just as much dilettantes) who have never inspected an old instrument, let alone played one, who know but a very minute and unimportant fragment of the music, and who know nothing but what Landowska tells them. I have found possibly two exceptions to this uninteresting lot of teadrinkers.

November 10, 1931

Thursday it poured buckets. I was told that was an excellent sample of a Parisian winter. I shall resort to an umbrella, if there is a continuance of the present efficiency of my raincoat in forming a collecting reservoir between my shoulder blades. I stood around outside Notre Dame, watching the spouting gargoyles, while waiting for Hubert and Lydia, and after their arrival, waiting to get in for the Berlioz Requiem. We got seats in the tribune of the crossing, where we could look across both transepts and down the choir into the apse, with its marvelous perspective of flaming windows and Gothic arches. The service, most impressive, was for the Colonial dead. It was not stated whether that meant the Frenchmen who were eaten by cannibals or died of yellow fever, or whether it meant the people that the French killed. However, it was perfectly gorgeous. In the very center of the crossing was a black catafalque surrounded by tall white candles, and on all four sides great brass torches burning with a clear blue flame. Behind that there was an altar, and twenty or thirty bishops and cardinals dressed in magnificent robes. The Berlioz setting of the Requiem text, although theatrical to the utmost, was done with a subtlety and a degree of musical quality that I had not expected.

I worked at harmony rules until I was ready to throw the book out the window; then I did finger exercises. (Promising young artist spends a day in inspiring activity.) In the afternoon I went out to St. Leu for a lesson with Landowska. More than an hour of that woman and her all-pervasive personality makes me ready to go crazy. And she is very nice to me, but she wants to make me simply a part of her own ego, and have complete control over me, a thing which I constantly resist, an exhausting process. And I have already expressed my opinion of most of the other pupils. She is not a good teacher in that she does not explain things well, or discuss anything whatever. There is absolutely no question of doing anything but what one is told. Any exercise of personal intelligence is not considered necessary and is ignored. Like many artists she has two completely separate aspects, what she does and what she says. She talks a great deal about principles and reasons, but practically, she acts on her own personal taste, as do most artists. However, I shall go through with it for the sake of the technic.

Last night was the first of the Beethoven concerts by the Lehner Quartet, beautifully played, especially the slow movements. The subtlety of variation and color in a string quartet is one of the most wonderful things in all music. There is a strange affinity in tone quality with the clavichord, sustained tone excepted.

Tuesday, November 17, 1931

Landowska gave me a very good lesson, helping me on a number of important points. She also said I had improved, because I played better for her than last week. However, I am beginning to notice an increase in strength and control in my fingers.

November 23, 1931

This afternoon I went to St. Leu, where considerable improvement was manifest in my fingers, according to Landowska, but I cannot say that during the entire afternoon I heard from anyone, myself included, any playing that revealed a vestige of musical beauty.

December 1, 1931

In the evening I went to hear Gieseking in a program of Bach and Debussy. He plays Bach with the most marvelous clarity and serenity of anyone I have ever heard. In a fugue, for example, all the voices are laid out with the utmost clarity, so that following the music (in

73

case it is unfamiliar) is completely superfluous. He plays Bach in a very limited range of dynamics, never very loud, but with the greatest subtlety and delicacy in phrasing, almost a true clavichord style, except that the piano never attains the clarity of the clavichord, and certain passages can never be heard on the piano. Gieseking's playing of slow movements has a marvelous contemplative serenity. Nearly all his playing has an ethereal intellectual "contemplative" effect because he almost never deals with strong physical rhythms. One nearly always is given a sense of motionlessness, quite different from the type of playing that exhilarates one by its physical rhythm and by its relation with the dance. Landowska's playing is the latter type, essentially rhythmic, with a precision that Gieseking almost never has, but without the serenity and fluid legato line of Gieseking's playing. When Gieseking plays a dance in a Bach suite, for example, it is no longer a dance, but the spirit of a dance in thought, rather than a physically stimulating rhythm. It would be marvelous to be able to employ both these styles of playing.

I went out to St. Leu, and told my first lie to Landowska (probably the first of a long series). She renewed her invitation to St. Leu for Christmas, and I gulped, and hastily explained that I couldn't be sure, that it would be very nice, but that I probably would be traveling with friends in England. I wish I had said Germany. As a matter of fact, I may go to Chartres. I am not sure.

My playing showed improvement, and I endeavored to discuss several points of fingering and phrasing, with a most exasperating lack of success. I am not at all sure whether I should stay with her all winter, except for the fact that there is apparently no one else better here, and that she is giving a certain kind of technic.

The same afternoon I had the dreary pleasure of explaining to one of Landowska's pupils (of long standing, too) what a clavichord was, and of revealing to her that there were *three* in the room in which she has been at least four times a week for two years!

December 7, 1931

I was greatly pleased to meet M. Brunold,* since he is a harpsi-

* Paul Brunold (1875–1948), French musicologist and musician.

chordist of some reputation, the author of an excellent treatise on ornamentation, and the organist of St. Gervais, the successor of the Couperin family. Although he has little or no technic, I like the quality of his playing, particularly the charming way in which he interprets French harpsichord music, which is his specialty, and about which he apparently knows as much as anyone. I immediately made a decision, and asked him to give me some lessons, which he is going to do, beginning next Saturday. I explained to him that I was a pupil of Landowska, but he was most tolerant. Landowska would be furious if she knew about this, because she hates him. However, he is going to be a most valuable supplement to her. I am particularly glad to find him because he is a friend of Dolmetsch, and has an attitude toward the harpsichord with which I am much more sympathetic than with Landowska's. He will be very tolerant, and in many ways much more helpful. Since I met him, the musical horizon seems to have extended itself in a very welcome way.

My technic (Landowska's style) has really made good progress. My fingers are much stronger and more even and, I find, now very well adapted to Mozart, although I still feel that my Mozart playing is quite dead. However, with this has come a strong tendency toward stiffness, which I must combat.

December 14, 1931

I went over to Pleyel's to practice the harpsichord. In the studio they had one of their early models of harpsichords, which, although it had a wooden frame, was even worse than the present ones. In addition, it was about as much in tune as a mouse trap. However, for two hours I ground out finger exercises and Bach (Wanda's version, which might just as well be practiced on a barbed wire fence, for all its musical qualities).

I went to Gabriel Gaveau's and practiced their harpsichords. The tone in most of the stops is infinitely superior to that of the Pleyel, but the construction is somewhat sloppy, and the mechanism quite poor. The low notes are very poor. But it is the best thing I have found here. I despair of ever locating a good harpsichord in Paris! I worked on some Chambonnières and Couperin for Brunold. So far,

I have not gotten into the spirit of French harpsichord music very satisfactorily.

Saturday morning I saw Mr. Brunold. His ideas about harpsichord playing are very close to mine, which under Landowska I have been forced temporarily to suspend. His tone is infinitely superior to hers. If I can combine her precision and rhythm with a suppleness and beauty of tone, the resulting system, in ideal at least, ought to be fairly satisfactory. He owns a tremendous amount of material on French harpsichord music, and is going to let me work with some of it, and even borrow some, which will be helpful. Tomorrow night I go to his house, which will be most interesting.

The week previous he had passed a remark about Landowska's having altered the shape of the harpsichord to that more like the piano in order that the audience might see her hands. Later at Pleyel's I had occasion to verify that statement, while I was practicing on their early model, which had the traditional square ends enclosing the keyboard, when I noticed a hook at my right. I investigated and found that the right side (the side always toward the audience) was hinged and could be opened out and fastened back! The other side, being unimportant, was untouched. This little discovery amused me very much as additional insight into Landowska's psychology.

I wrenched myself out of bed and over to Mlle. Boulanger for the lesson which she had not been able to give me on Friday. She was quite encouraging about the counterpoint. I hope to be able to finish up two-part counterpoint by the first of January. She didn't get through all the harmony. I find it difficult to turn her off sometimes, when she starts talking about irrelevant subjects. She had just come from Berlin, where she was one of the judges in a contest for young composers, and had some very interesting things to say about Germans and German music, as she saw them, from a French point of view. However, she is to a certain extant conscious of the impossibility of French and Germans ever understanding each other. She felt that the Germans were terribly restless and were desperately groping about musically and otherwise. She thought they had lost peace and pure beauty, the eternal remark of a Latin race about a Germanic race. She was shocked by the books in Berlin bookshops!!

76

I think she will be distressed when she finds that I want to go to Germany. I am afraid I am in all respects pretty much a Germanophile. However, I ought to go and see before I settle down. I would consider going to Germany for Christmas if it didn't threaten to reduce the travel budget to the point of eliminating the trip to Italy in the spring.

This evening was most important. I visited M. Brunold, who made me a number of revelations. He played me his beautiful old clavichord (I must have one) in a most enchanting style, although I don't approve of his system of touch. The glory of the evening was his magnificent harpsichord, an instrument of the early 18th century, very well restored and with a marvelous richness of tone, one of the very best I have ever heard. The case was very beautiful, too, with a charming landscape painted on the lid and flowers scattered over the sounding board. He played Couperin on it in a fashion which revealed things I had never suspected in the music, and he produced some marvelous effects with the instrument. Although his interpretation is sometimes a little too romantic, I think, and his constant shifting of the tempo frequently oppressive, he is thoroughly imbued with the spirit of the music, from having lived with it all his life, and he makes it come alive in a rare fashion. Although he plays the harpsichord much like the piano and a bit sloppily, he knows how to produce a most beautiful tone in a variety and subtlety that Landowska never dreamed of, and that I had never realized so much. But on the other hand, he has not her clarity and precision. Oh, for the combination!

After the harpsichord, I was granted another wish of long standing: to hear a forte piano of Mozart's time, well restored to playing condition. He had a beautiful English table piano, with a most interesting history, having belonged to the Cardinal de Rohan. It is a revelation to hear Mozart and early Beethoven on it, and quite changes one's ideas of their interpretation. It is a kind of cross between the modern piano and the clavichord. The tone quality is infinitely better adapted to the music. The primitive nature of the action makes necessary a species of touch very close to the old-fashioned Clementi finger technic, and other schools which have since persisted in applying to the modern piano the technic of 1780.

I think I see the origin of Landowska's technic somewhere here, originally related to the original instruments which Mozart played, and not at all to those she uses.

December 25, 1931

Through Mlle. Boulanger, we got into the rehearsal, Thursday morning, for the Stravinsky concert. It was most interesting, and rather exciting to see what Stravinsky is like personally. We found, when we came in, rehearsing the Fire-Bird Suite, a slim sleek fellow in sweater and plus-fours, looking from a distance for all the world like a soda clerk in an ice cream parlor! But after that, he is a man of tremendous vitality, which one felt particularly in his conducting of his own music. His performance of the Fire-Bird was particularly illuminating in contrast to Koussevitsky's to which I am accustomed. With Stravinsky one heard entirely different things in the score, and more the piece as a whole rather than Koussevitsky's emphasis on detail. Stravinsky's interpretation is extremely broad and simple, like his later music, and quite unlike the music of Fire-Bird itself. I suspect that at the time he wrote it (nearly twenty years ago) he would have conducted it more like Koussevitsky with a very romantic spirit. But now he has developed so far away from it that his conception is entirely different.

In connection with old music, I was newly reminded by seeing all this music fresh from the workshop and still in the composer's hands, how ridiculous it is for some people to be too dogmatic about the "correct" or ideal interpretation of old music, when so often the original performances (as in the Violin Concerto) are far from perfect presentations of the works, or when composers perform quite differently from their indications in the scores.

Saturday morning I got myself out of bed and braved the bitter cold to practice at Gaveau's before my lesson with Brunold. He is refreshingly tolerant. Although there is much in his playing that I don't like, he can capture the spirit of the music in a way that I have never heard. By the combination of his own registration and my ideas, we worked out a delicious registration of "Le Carillon de Cythère." I find him particularly stimulating in problems of registration, because he is an organist, on Couperin's own instrument, and because he has such an intimate acquaintance with the possibilities of a good, old harpsichord.

I forgot to mention in connection with Landowska, that she spoke again about the desirability of getting me a fellowship (and her more money!). I don't know what she thinks I have now, but I don't mind her ignorance. She spoke mysteriously of a letter from Mrs. Coolidge, and how "we would talk about my career next time!" If this continues, one way or another, it is bound to be extremely embarrassing. If Landowska got someone "interested" in me, which I think improbable, she would howl with rage at my "ingratitude" when I deserted her and many of her ideas. On the other hand, these discussions about my future have to be managed very carefully on my part!

January 4, 1932

The course at St. Leu this afternoon was more interesting, and more musical than usual. Somebody played a noble suite from Handel on which Landowska did some very interesting work. She has now started me on the Well-Tempered Clavichord. (More sheep for the slaughter!) I was somewhat pleased to be told of my unusually quick improvement by one of the other pupils (Professor of Harpsichord "Method Wanda Landowska" at the Conservatory at Geneva) who had heard me early in the fall. But I was equally surprised and shocked to hear her asking if the pedals on an organ had more than one stop!

January 11, 1932

Landowska was very affable, this afternoon, gave me some peculiar fingering and phrasing, remarked on the rapid development of my hand, etc., and continued on the subject of finding me a patron, a subject which, under the circumstances, I should prefer to avoid. Apparently she does not know about the Paine fellowship. Probably so much the better. But she wants to make it possible for me to stay beyond June, and it is evident that before writing to Mrs. Coolidge, she is trying to extract some sort of declaration of allegiance from me. Naturally these things do not always keep me restrained to Truth as well as Circumspection!

January 17, 1932

. . . Bibliothèque Nationale. That library is enough to give any American librarian white hair in two hours! There is a partial, published catalogue of old music. Then there are three accession catalogues 1882–1894, 1894–1922, 1922– arranged by subject in a so-far incomprehensible fashion, composed of little slips of paper bound in books. For some material prior to 1882, there are photostats of the old catalogues. The Author catalogue only goes up to M! Hence there are large sections of which catalogues are not accessible to the public. It certainly would be a good deed for some American millionaire to supply some of these European libraries the wherewithal to make a good card catalogue.

January 25, 1932

In the evening I went to the harpsichord concert of Pauline Aubert, the same woman who put on a terrible concert of two harpsichords in the fall. It was in an excellent small hall, and the instrument was a Dolmetsch-Gaveau, possibly the best I have ever heard. In the first number, probably because of nervousness, Mme. Aubert gave what I expected, but after that her playing was positively ravishing. She played Couperin with the most subtle restraint and delicacy, and some Rameau, some French sonatas with flute, one of the Kuhnau Bible Sonatas. Her registration was simple but beautifully chosen and most effective. Her phrasing was sensitive and supple, with ornaments played with a superb grace. Her technic occasionally included some false notes and occasionally one felt a slight lack of vigor in her playing, but her interpretations all possessed a restraint and objectivity that made the fullest effect in a piece after it was finished, a very rare quality in any musician, and admirable for most harpsichord music. When she began the extremely realistic Kuhnau narrative sonata on David playing the harp before Saul, I was amused by the vividness of her interpretation, but I ended by taking the piece seriously. When I think of the delicious effects and absolute blending that she obtained from that instrument in playing with the flute, my esteem of the Pleyel sinks even lower. All in all, it was a most inspiring concert.

80

February 9, 1932

. . . the Landowska concert at the Grande Salle Pleyel. I enclose the program. Musically, I was quite disgusted with the whole concert. The orchestra was dreadful and the Pleyel harpsichords do not blend well with strings. The concertos were rhythmically brittle and choppy, and filled with tricks of phrasing and registration that seemed in very bad taste. The slow movements were particularly brutally treated. The Partita, although technically nearly flawless, counted for nothing after the interpretation of it which I once heard from Gieseking. I really thought that one of my pupils this summer played with a much better style and interpretation (although I should admit that it was largely my own). I was much interested to observe the stage manners of Landowska, who appeared in a long velvet robe and glided on and off the stage in the most perfect manner. For each encore she approached the harpsichord with the air of a priestess again consenting to perform the sacred rite. It was really frightfully convincing! As little as possible was done during the evening to indicate that there was anything besides Landowska. The other harpsichords were at the back of the stage and the conductor meeky self-effacing, so that the red robe shone forth in its full glory.

After all this, I was much disturbed, and by Friday had decided to leave Landowska, but I since have decided that it would be better to follow through her system of technic until June, with all its disadvantages, since it is a rigorous training and will assure at least some sort of good foundation. Also in her teaching, one is kept dangling, driven almost to the point of leaving by several lessons in which practically nothing is given, then pulled back in by a lesson in which she gives valuable ideas. I am afraid that leaving at this midway point might be dangerous, although I spent most of last week thinking of excuses to get away.

Thursday I went out to St. Leu and listened to a lot of stage-business, including Landowska congratulating herself on the great concert.

In the afternoon I broached to Mlle. Boulanger the difficult subject of Germany. She made no attempt to advise me aside from harmony or counterpoint, except to advance the rather curious argument that although both French and Germans make bad editions of Bach, the French at least don't take them seriously and know they are bad because they are done in a hurry! She also remarked that a Frenchman would admit when he didn't know anything, which hardly seems to me more true than in any other country. She didn't seem to think that counterpoint‛was so important, and didn't expect me to study fugue, although I plan to. She thought, however, that the change in studying harmony was dangerous, that one should stick to one system, and expressed doubt that it was well taught in Germany, which latter seems unlikely. However, she was very fair and sympathetic and advised me to go to Germany if I thought that other considerations turned the balance.

After my lesson I practiced the harpsichord at Gabriel Gaveau's and passed a rather unpleasant two hours because of my mental disturbance and my complete dissatisfaction with what I was at the moment accomplishing with some very difficult pieces of Couperin.

Friday night I practiced for Landowska. Saturday morning I bicycled up to Gabriel Gaveau's for practice and for a rather more profitable lesson with Brunold, although it began rather inauspiciously by my pointing out some of the unpardonable defects of the instrument, of which he is not sufficiently critical from the point of view of mechanics and regulation.

In the afternoon I went out to St. Leu for a session as unprofitable as Thursday's session, for the most part. Landowska has a mortal fear of giving too much in her lessons.

The afternoon class out at St. Leu was unusually profitable. Probably there won't be another such for weeks. Landowska seemed to forget herself and become actually interested. She gave me some valuable ideas on the C sharp major Prelude of Bach, and actually talked about variety of harpsichord touch, something which I had despaired of hearing from her.

February 15, 1932

I went down to the Ile St. Louis for tea with the Curzons in their beautiful apartment with a Louis XV balcony, overlooking the river and one transept of Notre Dame. The living room had beautiful gray

Louis XV panelling and mantelpiece and a big satinwood harpsichord. We had a very interesting discussion about Landowska and our respective difficulties with her. She has been trying to "gyp" them in an incredibly dishonest fashion. They seemed to think her teaching and state of mind this winter to be far worse than ever before. We played for each other and were quite free with helpful cirticism. One of the pleasant features of the afternoon, as I afterwards realized, was that of being in a room that was entirely clean!

On the train out to St. Leu the Curzons showed me some very interesting programs given by the Dolmetsches in London this winter. Clifford Curzon played the piano in the class, with an extraordinary beauty of tone. He is apparently a concert pianist of considerable eminence in England. They are both pupils of Schnabel.

For the present, I apparently have Landowska turned off Bach onto Scarlatti.

Tuesday morning, counterpoint, afternoon practice at Pleyel's after which I went down to the Curzons for tea. I played the Chromatic Fantasy and had it torn to pieces in a very helpful way. I also played my old war horse the big A minor fugue, and demonstrated some theories about harpsichord touch.

February 22, 1932

In the afternoon I had a most unusual experience. Mlle. Boulanger gathered a large group of people to sing in her music-history class one of the motets of Tallis (died 1585) written in *forty* independent voice parts, eight choirs of five parts each. After a little work we sang it well enough to give a fair idea of the work, which is not only technically so extraordinary but musically very beautiful. The mere sound and fullness of the forty voices in chord progressions was gorgeous, and more so in connection with most effective silences and contrasting of a few voices with the whole ensemble. One of the most extraordinary features was the canonic entrance (i.e. in imitation) of all forty parts successively. I don't suppose that I shall ever hear this again, as in America it is so difficult to gather forty people capable of singing each a rather difficult independent part.

I was not very favorably impressed with Mlle. B.'s lecturing in this class, because the time passed with rather little said, and there was an abundance of dangerous generalizations and slipshod statements.

The major event which I have to relate occurred later in the afternoon at the Société Française de Musicologie, where I purposely arrived late, as my name was being proposed for membership. I found Brunold getting ready for his paper and *Landowska* evidently sitting in the seat of the scornful, eyeing him through a large lorgnette! My amazement increased when I saw her go up and speak to him at the end of the meeting, as they are by no means friendly and a bitter argument was pursued in a periodical some years ago. Brunold said afterwards that she was very agreeable on this occasion, which seemed particularly strange to me in view of the subsequent information that I had been introduced to the meeting as *Brunold's Pupil*! Although I have been preparing to face a terrible scene with L., the whole thing strikes me as terrifically funny! I got all braced for the scene this afternoon, but curiously enough, Landowska was most agreeable and gave no indication of knowing about what had happened. It is barely possible that she arrived late to the meeting, or else she prefers to hang on to her pupils.

February 29, 1932

Late in the afternoon I went out to Boulogne-sur-Seine to hear Miss Swainson* play her clavichord. It was a beautiful Dolmetsch instrument, better than the one in Cambridge. She played beautifully, producing an amazing variety of effects, many of which I had not discovered. She is a pupil of Dolmetsch and renews my conviction that there is a great deal to be gotten from him. He told her an amusing story, which I do not believe, of Landowska's visit to Haslemere! It seems that she brought a secretary to take notes on some information which she wanted from him. The main feature of the story however is that he played the clavichord to her, and felt himself especially inspired on the occasion, and finished the Chromatic Fantasy to find her in tears at his feet! Afterwards she resumed her professional mask and went away. — — — I hope that by becoming

---

* Dorothy Swainson

84

a harpsichordist I won't become such a liar as most of my colleagues!

I was much pleased, in playing Miss Swainson's clavichord, that although I have hardly touched the instrument since June, I have gained enormously in finger control and equality.

March 14, 1932

This week has been rather turbulent, following my visit to Gaveau's last Tuesday, where Brunold was putting the finishing touches on the harpsichord. M. Gaveau continued to insist on my renting one of his lousy pianos, and on my refusal, in turn refused to send the harpsichord on the following day. Naturally I was furious and very much disappointed, after my long wait and lost time. However, I went to see Brunold who was very nice, and even offered me the use of his beautiful old instrument. Now the matter is fortunately straightened out, and the harpsichord is really due to arrive at eleven o'clock Wednesday morning.

March 21, 1932

At last the harpsichord is here and I can hardly keep away from it long enough to do anything else. It is mechanically much better than the other one on which I have been practicing, and the tone is very fine, with tremendous resonance. Although it has been slightly out of tune since the moving, and some of the quill stops show signs of variability, it is very satisfactory to work on. And it is so wonderful for the first time to have a harpsichord so completely at my disposal.

Hôtel de Solesmes à Solesmes
March 27, 1932   par Sablé (Sarthe)

Yesterday I worked on my various projects, took a short bicycle ride in the sunshine, and went to tea with Mrs. Curzon. We had an interesting discussion of harpsichord affairs. She is going to Berlin next week and will find out all she can for me. She took a lesson with Pauline Aubert and found her miserably disappointing, with even more ballyhoo than Landowska. I wonder why her concert was so impressive to me.

April 18, 1932

At noon I received a note from Miss Swainson, inviting me to come to her house to meet Mr. Dolmetsch! I found a humpshouldered little old man with long scraggly white hair and a thin gray beard and wizened face with sharp, brilliant brown eyes. He is in some respects decidedly warped, to the point of craziness, and said many foolish things, but he does know a great deal and admits it to be only a small fraction of potential knowledge, although he is conceited to the utmost and will tolerate no disagreement. But his egoism and his "shouting down the world" differ from Landowska in that they are directed more at a cause than at personal glory, and they seem to be perfectly honest. An unfortunately large part of the afternoon was spent on musical gossip and histories of his more famous quarrels, and various assertions of his capabilities and those of his family.

He played the clavichord with an extraordinary variety and beauty of tone color, although marred by lapse of memory and the assertion that there is only one way to play a piece and he can prove why!

I think that there will be opportunity for me to learn a great deal at Haslemere this summer, in spite of the crazy people with whom I shall be working!

Wanda, noticing the enormous improvement in my playing and realizing that I had been using a harpsichord more, asked me where I had been practicing. For far from innocent reasonings I told the truth! If I had said I was still practicing at Pleyel, she would have been nasty enough to inquire. She took it fairly well, however, but told me I had done wrong not to ask her advice and that as her pupil I should rely entirely on her, and that she was much surprised at this lack of trust, and that none of her other pupils would do such a thing, but perhaps in America it was different, but didn't I understand? − etc. for half an hour. I explained my point of view (cautiously!) and said I understood how she felt but I couldn't feel that way, whereupon she said, "You must think over what I say, because the things I say are likely to be profound"!! And so it went, but she didn't seem very displeased, even when I got to the point of explaining that I didn't like the Pleyel harpsichord. I was led into that by a long and devious train. When she first saw me she asked me what had turned up for staying with her. I thought quickly of the possibility of Professor Hill having written her the truth about the fellowship renewal, put on a very pleased air and said that I had been enabled to stay till July 1. After more questions it hastily developed that no, it wasn't family but friends — in New York! Then I must have a harpsichord to take back to America with me, — more stalling around up to the point afore-mentioned. And so it goes. I am getting rather tired of the mental strain involved in keeping straight all the various maneuvers. I agree heartily with Montaigne when he says that the liar has a hard life because of the difficulty of remembering all his prevarications! I shall be very glad to resume a simple — and truthful life!

April 25, 1932

This afternoon I went out to St. Leu, finding Landowska very agreeable and the quality and value of her teaching considerably improved. It seems that I am to play a Handel Suite for the big "cours d'inauguration" June 4.

Tomorrow night is the first Furtwaengler concert with the Berlin orchestra. It will be good to hear a good orchestra again.

May 3, 1932

I went to a "Festival Haydn" in the Salle Pleyel, directed by Cortot, who, I hope, is a better pianist than conductor. Landowska played a Haydn piano sonata quite pleasingly, and the D major harpsichord concerto really very well, with a brilliance of registration and a clarity and precision that succeeded in making its effect on me, even if, on account of the abominable acoustics, I was hearing every note twice! She played her own cadenzas, which I avow were *not* so good! Her stage manners were, as usual, very amusing. She had a huge popular success and glided on and off the stage for bows as if she were on wheels, walking with arms tight at her sides, reminding me of Mrs. Lowell's saying that on the stage she always looked like a trained seal!

Monday I practiced and went out to St. Leu. Landowska's instruction has picked up amazingly in musical value. I know it is not only myself, but I can notice it with all the others in the class.

le 10 Mai, 1932   München

I went out to St. Leu for Landowska's Bach concert. Landowska glided on stage and with a soulful expression played the first line of the Passion chorale and then gave a rather unappealing performance of the A minor English suite and two Preludes and Fugues. Then she gave a really delightful interpretation of the "Capriccio on the Departure of a Brother," and two really admirable Preludes and Fugues and a superb performance of the Italian Concerto that quite swept me off my feet. It was really the first time I had ever heard her play so well. When she does play well, one feels a marvelous quality, but when she doesn't, her playing is very offensive, most curious extremes.

[*Encouraged by Mlle. Boulanger to take a short holiday, I had accepted an invitation from a fellow student to drive to Munich. We left Paris on May 6th by way of Nancy and Strasbourg, stopping in various cathedral towns as we passed.*]

As we left Soissons we began to see traces of trenches and occasional piles of barbed wire in the fields, almost unnoticeable in the fertile, sunny countryside.

Entering Reims, we saw the towers of the cathedral white above the town showing from a distance little trace of damage. The town itself is not at all the pathetic ruin that I had imagined, but rather has a prosperous liveliness and a certain rich feminine air that carries the atmosphere of the cathedral even to the modern buildings. After having heard so much about the pathetic state of the cathedral I was pleasantly surprised to find remaining even still so much that is wonderfully beautiful. From a distance one ignores the terrible scars of the west front in seeing the marvelous harmony of proportion and perfection of ensemble that make it to my mind the most beautiful façade in France. Unlike Amiens and Paris, one does not regard the façade as a screen somewhat unconnected with the rest of the building, because one finds in the exterior indications of the division and light of the interior nave and aisles, and of the height of the roof. The carving on the interior of the west front also makes a transition from the elaborate sculpture of the exterior to the austerity of the interior nave.

As one approaches nearer the cathedral, one sees how much detail has been carried away from above the porches and how terribly calcined the stone of the north side became during the burning of the scaffolding, so that some carving is almost entirely obliterated. The portals, especially the central and south, although without their rose windows, preserve their sculpture almost untouched. The sculpture has little of the severity of Chartres or even Amiens, but is mostly soft and feminine, often even coquettish, although certainly not lacking in majesty.

St. Rémy we found in an even more lamentable state than the cathedral, with nearly all the vaulting fallen in, all the roof gone, staring ambulatory windows with fragments of stained glass hanging in them, workmen and trucks in the interiors among broken altars and the weatherbeaten marble shrine still loaded with sandbags, vaulting keystones and fragments of sculpture, and even a huge contrabass leaning against a wheelbarrow!

[My companion having already noticed in Strasbourg that I was more interested in architecture than in her, we separated on arriving in Munich. I visited the German harpsichord makers in Munich and in the still gloriously intact Nürnberg, and frequented the Alte Pinacothek and the Opera, hearing *Freischütz* for the first time. Next to Mozart it remains my favorite German opera. I still feel shivers down my spine in the Wolf's Glen scene! I returned to Paris by way of an unforgettable week in North Italy, over the Brenner to Verona, Padua, Venice and afterwards Milan. I omit my descriptions of this trip because unfortunately they convey little of what was in fact one of the overwhelming experiences of my life.]

June 7, 1932   21 Rue Jacob, Paris

The "Cours Publique" was much better than I had expected, Landowska giving many valuable suggestions and comments to the pupils as they played. She also played to illustrate her points, or improvised counterpoints at a second harpsichord while the pupils played. She seems to be an entirely different person from what she was in the winter. This is not merely my own imagination, because the Curzons also remarked on it. Now, when she plays a Bach concerto, there is an air of vitality and splendor that hangs over the whole thing. It is a most extraordinary transformation! Her teaching is incomparably better and she gives much more than before to all the pupils. There were other less creditable features, such as the fact that her harpsichord was arranged to have a much better sonority than that on which the pupils played, and that she supplemented the real superiority of her own playing by many illegitimate means which produced their desired effect on the public, but which were rather obvious to those acquainted with the harpsichord.

13 Juin 1932   Paris

I rode back in the train with Putnam Aldrich, whom I have possibly mentioned as having studied with Landowska for two years, and playing in America this year, and now returning for the summer. I knew him at Concord.

Monday night, June 20

I won't say any more about him as I am practicing not saying nasty things about my compatriot harpsichordists! However, it suffices to say that he married one of Landowska's secretaries, and that he is a diligent follower of Landowska.

In the winter I wrote a letter to Mr. Surette in which I gave some account of my work and my reactions, with the expectation of having its contents intelligently interpreted and discreetly guarded, which does not seem to be the case. It seems that true to usual practice he has been broadcasting secondhand generalizations about Landowska. (Now I mustn't be so nasty, as he has been very convenient! But my respect for him with age and perspective has been undergoing some reevaluation.) At any rate Mr. Surette said to Aldrich, "What are you going back to France for, to teach Landowska? It seems she needs it," all of which was speedily reported to Landowska! At least this is what Aldrich tells me, for some unknown reason. It seems that she was going to make a terrible scene, but so far she has said nothing, and has seemed indifferent. However, I find Aldrich in a way rather convenient for conveying to Landowska various things that I would rather like her to know but prefer not to tell her directly! It seems that practically everything I say is quickly retailed, because I can nearly always see evidence of it in

Landowska's attitude at the next class! Today, for example, was a long sermon against the clavichord, the result of my having spoken of it to Aldrich! All this is rather amusing, although it does not make me any more comfortable or feeling "among friends" at St. Leu. However, the high state of disfavor to which I have arrived does not seem to affect the quality of the lessons. Also I have to tell fewer falsehoods because the air is somewhat cleared and because I am now asked fewer embarrassing questions!

June 27, 1932

I was unwise enough to go to a Chopin recital played by Paderewski, who is now nearly eighty. It was most pathetic and at times painful to be cooped up in a concert hall with a French piano and the remains of genius. In some of the technically easy pieces one caught glimpses of really beautiful playing, but for the most part the concert was a painful exhibition of exaggerated romantic mannerisms and false notes by the handful, and a style shorn by age of most of its refinement. Aside from the degeneration of control the poor man no longer has the physical strength for many passages. But always one tended to be more conscious of pianism than of music. It also seemed regrettable to see an old artist who ought to possess a marvelous mature serenity as a result of age vainly trying to warm over the unrest and romantic passions which make much of Chopin essentially the music of youth.

I must stop now and practice, as I go to St. Leu tomorrow. Meanwhile I wonder what new trouble my "friend" Aldrich has cooked up for me with Landowska! Oh, *that woman*!!

July 6, 1932

Last week I was going to tell about the Cortot course, which proved so interesting. Cortot, although I don't particularly care for his playing of Beethoven, has a very intelligent approach and a very sound musical conception of the sonatas, which rests more or less untouched by Gallicisms of interpretation. He is a careful and sympathetic teacher. It was such a contrast after St. Leu to see the pupils treated courteously and sympathetically with a respect for their own mental processes, and to see a compete lack of showmanship and self-glorification. He is the perfect type of Frenchman, it seems to me, refined to the utmost, with the characteristic French sensibility of emotion and clarity of thought. It was a delight to hear him speak such beautiful clear and refined French. Withal, his conceptions of the music by no means equal the actual grandeur of the conceptions of Beethoven. There is always something lacking. His art, like most French music, seems a hothouse product, delicately flourishing in one corner of the human spirit, with none of the wholehearted surge of German music, nor the roots in the soil of popular dance and song. The courses were admirably prepared. Each executant was required to submit a detailed analysis of his sonata, some account of its origin, and remarks upon his conception of the interpretation. Aside from its value in clarifying the ideas of the student, the teacher is prepared to understand what the pupil is aiming at, even if unsuccessfully.

July 10, 1932

I went to St. Leu, feeling quite uncomfortable, and dreading the afternoon, to find Landowska in a most expansive and inspired mood. I played some Handel pieces which went fairly well. Landowska played several times during the course of the afternoon very beautifully, and finally carried us all away completely by her playing in a lesson on a Haydn piano sonata. I have never heard anything like it in the world. She is certainly a pure genius when it comes to Haydn and Mozart. One is inclined to forgive her character when with one phrase, she can transport an audience into a perfect paradise.

Haslemere, Surrey
July 19, 1932   [I had left Paris on July 14]

In the afternoon I went out to St. Leu. There Landowska sprang what I had been expecting. She called me up in her room and went off on a long and embarrassing tirade on the subject of my letter to Mr. Surette. I am sorry I haven't a record of all the extraordinary things she said, but among them was something like this: "How can you expect to comprehend the mystery and complication of that phenomenon which is Wanda Landowska?" At this point the dog came in and committed an indiscretion! – On such occasions I always have what the French nicely term "l'esprit de l'escalier," that is, I never think of the right things to say until afterwards too late. Anyway it was obvious that no explanation would ever make her understand my point of view. However, she demanded that I write a letter of apology for my faithlessness as a pupil, etc. I have not written yet, because I do not know exactly what to say, but I intend to write some kind of an explanation that all I demand from her is criticism in lessons, which is paid for in good solid French francs, and that I feel no other obligations. Naturally I shall state the case more tactfully. I think that I might have been upset by this if I were younger, and if I did not know that this happens with nearly all her pupils. The only really annoying part is in case I decide that I want to study with her some more, or in case she writes, as she threatened, goodness knows what to Professor Hill. I have not really made up my mind about her, since the summer when she has been showing so much more to give, that I wonder if I shouldn't go back. On the other hand I never really enjoy working with her and my intense dislike of her takes a great deal away from what she has to give musically, aside from the fact that in many respects I can never feel the same way musically.

[I had left Paris for England on July 14, pausing to make an expedition through Normandy, partly by bicycle and partly by train. I stopped at Bayeux, Caen (my first revelation of what Romanesque without Richardson could be!), St. Lô, Coutances, Mont St. Michel, and embarked at St. Malo for Southampton by way of Jersey. I omit also the account of my first visit to London.]

Tuesday evening was a concert of English chamber music with some extraordinarily fine pieces for the viols. The Dolmetsch family is a funny lot. Mr. Dolmetsch plays the violin, descant viol, recorder, lute, harpsichord, all about equally badly. His clavichord playing is a little better. The programs are marvelous, and the performances on the whole pretty terrible exhibitions of satisfied mediocrity, and usually worse. Landowska may be criticized, but she does *well*. The Dolmetsches seem perfectly satisfied if they can simply get through a piece. Anything better seems to happen by luck! Of course, it is remarkable to find a family so devoted to one activity and able to do anything at all with their musical point of view and the fact that they each play half a dozen instruments on which they practice very little. But they really ought to stick to research and the construction of instruments, with someone else to do the playing.

July 28, 1932

But now I am beginning to wonder which is more difficult to deal with, Landowska or Dolmetsch! I implore you, if I ever get like that, either to beat it out of me or to seclude me at the bottom of a pond in the company of a millstone! However, it is really more Dolmetsch's strongly ingrained ideas and a certain senile mental degeneration rather than his personal character that make him difficult. I went up to see him the other night, and he raved away about the terrible things in Paris, and told me I couldn't do anything until after the Festival and that the principal way to musical education was by listening to his concerts before doing anything oneself, etc. (I thought, "Yes, by way of warning.") . . . The difficulty of the situation is that I don't want to take lessons in playing (neither can I afford it) from any of them, except possibly a few clavichord lessons from the old man because he produces such beautiful sonorities from the instrument, although his playing generally is pretty much of a mess. . . . What I really want is access to the instruments and to information via the old man's marvelous library and conversation with him purified (the impossible!) of all irrelevant digressions. Mrs. Dolmetsch* is very kind, and apparently the most accessible of the lot. I hope to find out a lot about old dances from her, as she has spent much time reviving them.

The concerts have been of varying degrees of quality. Rudolph's** harpsichord playing reveals an unexpected amount of technic, but a nondescript character and complete rhythmic spinelessness, which was particularly in evidence in some of the pieces that I had heard Landowska play. We have been afflicted with Cécile*** on every

---

* Mabel Dolmetsch (1874–1963), the author of important books on Renaissance dance
** Rudolph Dolmetsch (1906–1942)
*** Cécile Dolmetsch (1904–)

program, Monday being the prize night, when she sang and played the rebec at the same time, accompanied by her father on the lute, with never any agreement in pitch between voice or either instrument. Although some of the violin playing has been pretty awful, the lowest depths were reached yesterday in the Bach D minor concerto for two violins, of which I never hope to hear a more frightful performance.

Sunday, August ?, 1932

Possibly the most important event has been my decision to revoke my order for the old German clavichord, and instead to take one of the Dolmetsch instruments. The instrument that I am to have is just being finished. Mrs. Dolmetsch is going to paint it in tempera for me, the outside a very dark blue green, the interior in a light gray blue-green such as one sees in old Italian instruments, something like clove-pink leaves, aquamarine, or seawater, with gold lettering and bands.

Monday

Last night's "little clavichord playing" protracted itself far into the night, and with the idea that I am beginning really to be able to play the instrument, gave me so much encouragement that I returned immediately to the instrument this morning. It still amazes me that such a tiny and simple instrument seems to offer no limit to its possibilities for shading and color. I find that I am able to play on these Dolmetsch clavichords great quantities of music that have never before sounded well on the clavichord. For the sake of my recent decision, I hope, and am fairly sure, that this is due more to the superiority of the instruments than to the gain in my own skill.

However, I hardly feel sure of anything I have achieved on the clavichord. It is all so delicate that it seems almost to be blown away by the slightest misgiving or bad balance.

The advent of the clavichord to my room was the result of a discussion with Mr. Dolmetsch, in which I finally asked him for a lesson, which proved mildly profitable. The next (appointment at my choice, thank heaven!) will be more profitable, because I shall ask him about certain doubtful questions of ornamentation. I suppose that, eventually, to get at the harpsichords, I shall have to ask Rudolph for a lesson. Mr Dolmetsch is much less difficult than I had expected, and is really very kind, although he frequently goes off into tirades about the musical "imbeciles." He allows me to go to his house at any time to work in his library (another result of the clavichord lesson).

[What follows is taken from letters written in London, Paris and Berlin. I have rearranged my excerpts in order to correspond with the chronology of the actual events. I was in London principally for working in the British Museum.]

September 28, 1932   31 Upper Bedford Place, London
    My clavichord playing has improved considerably, and I am quite at home at the instrument. In a few months, I think, it will really be second nature to me.
    The Goldberg Variations are now memorized. Sunday night I played them for the Glovers after they had asked me to supper. However, they are still far from perfect, and nervousness plays havoc with them.
    I spent a delightful evening with Clifford Curzon, who played Farnaby, Mozart and Brahms for me, the latter particularly beautifully. He also reported that Schnabel in a recent lesson had spoken to him of Ramin as "a far greater harpsichordist than Landowska." Discounting racial prejudice, I found that information much in favor of coming to Berlin.

Paris — Bibliothèque Nationale
waiting for books (Oh, the heavy change!)
    Here I am in Paris, again marvelling at the inefficiency of French libraries, and recovering from my annoyance at being told to write a letter to the director for permission to see a Ms. piece of Rameau. If they would only divert some of the energy used in binding the public with red tape into proper cataloguing and reorganization of staff! To say nothing of substituting a little air for furniture polish and garlic in the reading room!

96

I saw a good deal of Elliott Carter,* much matured and stabilized, but very delightful, newly arrived at the Boulangerie. I went to see Mlle. Boulanger, who was very nice and gave me some letters to people in Berlin. My ears would burn at the nice things she said about me in these letters, if I did not suspect her of writing a dozen such a day!

October 24, 1932   Berlin

Wednesday evening I drank beer with the American composer Roger Sessions, to whom Mlle. Boulanger had given me a very nice letter. We had a very interesting conversation. I shall enjoy seeing more of him. Also I shall be interested to know his music, for he has possibly the foremost reputation here and at home, among American composers.

Last night I went to the Städtische Oper for a performance of "Die Entführung" of Mozart, a delicious opera, marvelously staged, with charming comedy, but musically a bit heavy. I am inclined to think Mr. Sessions was right in speaking of the heaviness of the North German as compared with the sparkle of the Austrian or Bavarian.

Mr. Sessions also expressed the opinion that Germany is tending toward decadence, a fact which will certainly come to pass, I think, unless she can stage a comeback from the disasters of the war against precautions that France and other countries have taken to prevent it and to keep Germany safely pushed down. I realized this first when the train passed dozens of idle factories and steel works, and again this afternoon in passing the great rich pre-war houses on the parks in Charlottenburg, shabby among drawn blinds, spotted with room-renting signs, or garish as hotels and dance-palaces. Berlin has not the air of a prosperous city, but I have been unable to fix upon the elements of that impression. Politically, everything seems quiet, the coming elections heralded only by posters and young men of various parties at street corners collecting in tin boxes funds for the campaigns.

* The distinguished American composer, a friend of RK's at Harvard, whose *Double Concerto* was written for RK and premiered by him in 1961.

Last night I heard a performance of *Götterdämmerung* at the Staatsoper, with the ever-magnificent Frieda Leider as Brunnhilde and a perfectly unspeakable "enrhumé" Siegfried. I cannot speak of the opera itself with entire admiration–splendid as is much of the music, my stay in France has possibly given me a little of the Latin love of brevity and conciseness. Dramatically, I think the "Ring" is a better argument in favor of the classical unities than all of Corneille or Racine. And how I loathe Siegfried as the type of the vague leaden-serious romantic hero who goes about doing things that no sensible person would want to do anyway! Also I am inclined to assign much of the music to the category of the *grandiose* rather than the *grand*.

30 Oktober, 1932   Leipzig

Last night I went around to the Thomaskirche to arrange for my lesson with Ramin, passing in the square a very impressive statue: JOHANN SEBASTIAN BACH scrawled in chalk below.

This morning I went to the service at the Thomaskirche, heard the cantata done with oboes probably just as out of tune from the cold as they were in Bach's time, enjoyed hearing many familiar chorales in the service.

Afterwards I had my lesson with Ramin, his very nice wife acting as interpreter at difficult spots. I played him about a third of the Goldberg Variations on a hideous Neupert harpsichord. He seemed pleased with some features, and made criticisms of the interpretation of certain variations and wanted more variety between each one in tempo, registration and touch. I could not tell how he ordinarily plays them because, not being in practice on them, those he played for me he did rather badly. Some of the ornaments were fantastically and indubitably wrong. I just realized it was because of the mistakes in the Bach-Gesellschaft text, which I corrected from the original edition. He will not be as exacting technically as Landowska, I think, but he has some interesting ideas about touch and registration, and will be infinitely more inspiring to work for. But why do these people use such dreadful instruments?! Although some of the Neupert harpsichords with wooden frames are delightful, most of the big concert instruments, I think, are perfect horrors.

98

7 November, 1932   Berlin

Monday was the Reformationsfest in Leipzig. I got to the Thomas-kirche just as a long line of women in black gowns with stiffly starched white caps were filing down the aisle. The expectations aroused by hearing sounds of trumpets and drums, and the organ modulating into D major were justified when the choir, much to my delight, began the opening fugue of the magnificent cantata "Ein Feste Burg," which we sang in the Bach festival. If the Lutheran church is the only Protestant church with decent music, it certainly makes up for the failings of the others. What superb hymn tunes!

In the evening I went out with . . . who reflects perfectly the superficial snobbism, mental flabbiness and parrot critical judg-ments of the professors to which I entrusted a portion of my edu-cation. My desire to meet some intelligent people rather than spongy-brained esthetes reminds me that I do not have the address of Saun-ders MacLane.

I have been practicing the harpsichord every morning at the Neu-pert agency, where there is a new instrument which pleases me very much. I have begun work on the Fifth Brandenburg Concerto, to my mind the best of all the harpsichord concertos.

I went to a harpsichord concert by Erwin Bodky, who played part of the Goldberg Variations (making me feel better about my own performance of them!).

I have found a very nice small Russian restaurant where I can get a three course meal for 50 pfennigs (twelve and a half cents!). Although they have seven names a week for Hamburg steak, the food is quite good, and the daily cabbage is a healthy diet. I get breakfast (hot milk and a couple of buns) for thirty pfennigs at a Trinkhalle (lunch cart) in the Hohenzollern Platz, so that I easily stay well under two marks (fifty cents) a day for food!

Yesterday I had lunch with Mrs. Harich-Schneider* and played her the Goldberg Variations on her Neupert harpsichord. She wants me to play them in December in a series of concerts of old music which she directs. If I feel that they are ready, I shall welcome the oppor-

---

* Eta Harich-Schneider (1897–), a distinguished harpsichordist, musicologist, and ethnomusicologist

tunity for experience and publicity. She also spoke about having me play the clavichord. She very kindly offered to let me practice on her harpsichord on the days when she is away from home teaching.

Last evening I went to a distinctly amateur performance of three of the Brandenburg Concertos. Although the performance was very sloppy and entirely lacked the rhythmic precision and unity that these works require, I found it useful for purposes of study. The Pleyel harpsichord sounds as much like a typewriter in Berlin as in Paris.

November 21, 1932   Berlin

If I ate my 50 pf "Deutsches Beefsteak" (yesterday known as Wiener Hackbraten, before that as Bitki, Gebäckt Macaroni (!) Tefteli, etc., today Russische Kotelett) this noon with more than usual relish, it was because I had celebrated the day by playing a large portion of the Goldberg Variations on Bach's own harpsichord in the Instrumentalmuseum in the Hochschule für Musik! Not only was the instrument interesting on account of its distinguished owner, but also because in general plan and musical satisfactoriness it is the finest old harpsichord I know. Although at present the quills are very weak and ill regulated, the instrument is still quite playable, with a mellowness of tone and a perfection of ensemble that make it a delight to play. There were fine harpsichords of Ruckers and Kirkman in the collection, also Weber's piano, still a most beautiful instrument, quite a revelation for the piano music of Weber, Beethoven or Schubert. Of a number of clavichords by distinguished makers the most satisfactory were two tiny portable instruments measuring about 1 x 3ft., but these, as everything else I have seen so far, are not comparable to my own clavichord, whether on account of age or bad restoration, I do not know.

I took two hours with Ramin, during which I played the rest of the Goldberg Variations and we went over the 5th Brandenburg Concerto and a Handel Chaconne. Ramin played a certain amount, with a great deal of vitality and a certain grand and very exciting style, along with many false notes and general indifference to detail. His playing is certainly that of a man of great talent, but distinctly personal, romantic and often rather restless.

100

December 1, 1932   Berlin
    Yesterday, harpsichord, and in the evening a concert of Bodky on
harpsichord and clavichord (an instrument the mere shadow of one
like mine). As usual, the program was superior to the performance.
Although I suppose there is possibly something laudable in a man's
being resigned to playing a piece slowly if he knows he can't play it
fast!

December 26, 1932   Berlin
    I had considered myself obliged to go to Leipzig for another
lesson with Ramin, and was quite relieved to have a note saying that
he had no time. I do not regret his departure for an American concert tour, as I cannot say that I have found that he had very much
to give, as perhaps you have already surmised.

January 24, 1933   Berlin
    I enclose the impressive looking program for the Goldberg Varia-
tions, which comes on Friday of this week. Although some of the
critics will be drawn to a new performance of "Salome" at the
Städtische Oper, I shall have definitely one from the "Vossische
Zeitung" and probably two or three others. Perhaps Mr. Sessions
will bring Klemperer, or be able through friends to scrape up some
more critics. I played the Variations last week to Mr. Sessions and
Mrs. Harich-Schneider and was considerably relieved of nervousness
by their approval. It will be a short program but quite enough for
real concentrated hearing, I think. I hope the harpsichord (which I
have not yet tried) will be fairly decent.
    Some weeks ago Mrs. Harich-Schneider received a letter from my
dear amiable teacher, Wanda Landowska, or rather dictated to her
secretary, warning her against me and demanding that I not be
allowed to appear in public. "Er sieht nett und harmlos aus, aber er
ist ein eingebildeter und unverschämter Emporkömmling." It occurred to me the other day to contrast these charming words with the
letter which Mlle. Boulanger gave me for Tiessen: "Charmant garçon,
fin, sensible et intelligent; *excellent* musicien" (which really was, I
admit, laying it on a little thick!). Wanda said nothing about me
musically, but told her secretary to say that she felt it her duty to

warn Mrs. Harich-Schneider against me, and that Wanda had taken steps to procure me a scholarship, that I had behaved in an any but grateful manner, and so on, for a whole page. At this rate, can you imagine what this dear lady is attempting to do for me in America! But I *implore* you to say *nothing* about it outside the family, on account of Putnam Aldrich who reports everything back to Landowska and who would thereby get Mrs. Harich-Schneider in trouble.

The Sessionses came to tea one Sunday and quite encouraged me by their enthusiasm over my clavichord playing. I have had two long evening talks with Mr. Sessions, over beer glasses, about German and French music, about Italy, about national consciousness, about New England countryside, about the dreadful prospect of going back to America and facing all the snobs and superficial dilettantes.

January 27, 1933

Sleep being yet impossible, I shall attempt to progress a little further on this letter with an account of the Goldberg Variations. I was not at all satisfied with my playing, but apparently the evening was a great success. The harpsichord turned out to be a perfect mousetrap of an instrument, and *no* joy to play. Yesterday evening I went to try it out and found no two octaves in tune. The variations, as I played some of them, sounded like a fantastic, nightmarish, Satanic caricature. As I arrived this evening, I found the tuner still at work on the instrument. Although I was not nervous before the audience, I felt quite uncertain with the instrument. *Five* critics were there, among the small but enthusiastic audience, four from Berlin papers, including Alfred Einstein, probably the most intelligent of the Berlin critics, and a man from the Associated Press! Mrs. Harich-Schneider gave an "interview" to the Associated Press man, and filled him full, that I was Landowska's best pupil, that I had a great future, etc., to which he replied that I *looked* talented! Professor Springer, another critic, was very enthusiastic, and told Mrs. Harich-Schneider that it was the best he had ever heard; I hope he *writes* something similar. Afterwards I talked with Einstein over the coffee. He was very nice to me, said he was surprised by my knowledge (painfully small yet) of old music, and invited me to his house on Monday. I anxiously await what he will write. Mr. Sessions was very nice.

However, I am considerably encouraged by the certainty that I am capable of playing much better than I did, and that in the future I can face the "anstrengend" task of playing forty-five uninterrupted minutes from memory, with more sureness.

March 9, 1933   Berlin
I am at the present moment enchanted with my new-grown command of German, which I discovered last week to carry me through *Egmont* without a dictionary, and which this week has absorbed me in *Wilhelm Meister*. Although I must qualify both works as respectively bad drama and novel, they contain such a wealth of stimulating ideas and sympathetic characters and sentiments that I prize highly my first real discovery of Goethe.

The Sunday after the concert I played the clavichord for a group of people gathered by Mr. and Mrs. Sessions. Unfortunately, most of the interesting, important or useful people were unable to come, but perhaps just as well, for I played very badly. However, I met considerable enthusiasm from a lady from Hamburg, whose family (so the Sessionses tell me) are prominent in Hamburg, were close friends of Brahms, and who are anxious to have me come and play privately in Hamburg, possibly laying the ground for concert engagements and possibly cementing a connection with the harpsichord-maker Glaser, that would secure me the use of an instrument (if I want it) while I am in Europe.

Lately I have seen Mr. Sessions rather more frequently. He has been very nice to me, and has suggested several interesting possibilities for concerts next year. He seemed to feel sure that if I went to Italy I could play in Venice and Rome, a most exciting prospect! He lent me his article on recent music in "Modern Music" which I read with new admiration of his powers of intellectual continuity and accurate generalization.

Last Saturday I had my trial with the clavichord in the radio station "Deutsche Welle". . . . The man to whom we had written had in the meanwhile been thrown out by the Nazis (I should say, "by the Government"!) and we were met by his successor, who had been given notice for Monday! He gave us little encouragement, on the grounds that Jews and foreigners are almost automatically counted

103

out, and that the new director of the music section is an ex-army-major, who, even if he knows anything at all about music, certainly never even heard of a clavichord! The interesting and profitable part of the afternoon was the making of wax records, which I afterwards heard, much to my astonishment and immense interest. It is such a curious sensation to hear oneself play. The same sentiments and feelings are aroused by the music that went into the playing of it, but the stimulus comes from without and one feels oneself moved like a string in sympathetic vibration. Although in nearly every case I was thankful that the records were not permanent, I was surprised by the real beauty of certain passages, as I was painfully dissatisfied with others. I noticed too a certain hotness and too great subjectivity in my playing that I should prefer to make in many cases nobler and more impersonal. I wish I had frequent opportunities to make records, for the opportunity of such wonderful ice-cold criticism is most welcome. The instrument itself sounds rather different on records, much amplified and astonishingly grandiose and brilliant, yet in many ways very satisfactory, much better than the harpsichord. If I were to make permanent records I should need to play in a special style, rather exaggerating nuances and carrying legato almost of the point of blurring.

The political situation and its outward manifestations here in Germany afford considerable interest. I don't know what proportion of truth percolates to America since Hitler called all the foreign newspaper correspondents together and under threat of deportation made clear what could and what could not be said. The change in Berlin newspapers in the past three weeks has been amusing, even if horrifying to witness. Certain pieces of propaganda appear so similarly in various newspapers, Nazi and otherwise, that they seem surely dictated from higher quarters. The caution with which the anti-Nazi papers (to avoid suppression) have conducted themselves is really funny. Any contrary sentiment or opinion is stated in the mildest terms and smothered with respectful references to "the Government" and to the "Chancellor." It happens that no one with whom I have talked has any doubt but that the Nazis managed the burning of the Reichstag themselves (there is death penalty for saying so!). Certainly the Communist party would not be so foolish as to cook their goose with the parliamentary desks and chairs, and the rumors of prepared poisoning of Berlin water mains and of dynamite, loudly broadcast in Nazi papers, offer a rather thin excuse for the complete extermination of the party. Of course the whole affair when properly followed up with propaganda and censorship was extremely successful. Now the young Nazis conduct tours through the ruined building.

In fact the turnover in government offices of all degrees has been really terrifying, with people of long established merit and reputation being thrown out in every direction. . . .

My impression of Hitler and the Nazis is extremely unfavorable. Hitler seems to be a son of a bitch of the first magnitude and a poor imitation of Mussolini. The Nazis represent a most detestable jingoism and trumpery, violent chauvinism and anti-semitism, militarism (although their parades seem to demonstrate an incapability of marching!), the apotheosis of the drug-store cowboy and the "petite bourgeoisie," that make the future rather black for Germany as a civilization of real culture and solidity.*

If the rumored post office censorship is being carried out with any thoroughness, this letter will certainly never reach you!

April 9, 1933   Weimar

On March 24 I played the clavichord in Mrs. H.-S.'s Collegium. I found it a rather annoying experience, being disturbed by the unaccustomed size of both room and audience and by the fact that the clavichord began to wobble away from me in the middle of the B flat Partita until a few programs under one leg saved the situation. As I warmed my hands up before the performance, in a small, resonant studio upstairs, the instrument sounded better than ever, and I played about ten times better than in the actual performance.

* Bernard Berenson's companion Nicky Mariano noted in her diary, "Vienna September 18th, 1933 . . . Here we have seen Kirkpatrick and Klemperer and have heard very furious anti-Nazi talk and glowing desire for war, revenge and destruction" (*Forty Years with Berenson*, London, 1966, p. 221).

Being obliged to plan on a return to America, I am led to consider my situation in a rather different light, namely the necessity of pointing up my morale and particularly my playing for an attack on America, even to the neglect of laying further foundations (theoretical work). I have attempted to work out a course of action, a program of letters to be written, personal influences to be cultivated, publicity, possibilities of earning money, programs, possible engagements, magazine articles, etc.

On this rather fertile ground fell the suggestion of Mrs. Harich-Schneider that it might be better not yet to go back to Paris and the cramping influence of the Paris musical atmosphere and theoretical studies, but to take advantage of the professional possibilities offered by Sessions for playing in Italy, and for choosing the very most inspiring and stimulating surroundings for my playing work, which now can be done anywhere there is a good harpsichord. I regarded the proposal with considerable suspicion, as I still do, and my conscientious conviction that I ought to be doing counterpoint exercises for Nadia is overcome only by the fact that the time would be so short anyway, and that such work would only be accomplished at the temporary expense of my practicing. Even more suspicious to my New England conscience (of which I am said to have the wrong kind) is the fact that it is really exactly what I should like to do! I talked a great deal about it with Roger Sessions, who seemed to think it the best thing to do, and who gave me and promised me letters to various people in Rome, Florence and Venice. . . .

I think I told you about the invitation to Hamburg, which I finally accepted. After several days of packing, I left Berlin on Tuesday, April 4, arriving in a maddeningly slow taxi at the station exactly one minute before train time, being put, clavichord and baggage, on the train by a miraculous porter, having an Italian grammar and a guide to North Italy thrust into my hand by Sessions, and waving farewells out the window, the unexcepted departure leaving me with exactly the same feelings of missing a train. It all happened so fast that even yet I do not feel as if I have really left Berlin! . . .

The von Beckerath family were delightful, and their house exceedingly pleasant. Mr. von Beckerath is a painter of considerable cultivation and, for his age, surprising consciousness of the new styles. Mrs. von Beckerath is a pianist, a charming, motherly, witty woman. Mrs. Predöhl, their daughter, sings. I did not meet the two sons, one of whom is a gamba and cello pupil of Grummer, and the other the builder of the new organ at Solesmes. Although it seemed so pleasant to be staying in a real tasteful house instead of rooming in a barber's family, what I found so very agreeable was the acquaintance with a family which has a background which none in our new America possesses, a family which in its successive generations has known Mendelssohn, Liszt, Joachim, Brahms, Reger, Hindemith, where the house overflows with the books and music of a century.

On Wednesday I . . . played before a dozen or so people, who were very enthusiastic. I played much better than on previous such occasions.

On Thursday I went to Lübeck, where I spent the entire day in the company of Günther Hellwig, whom I knew in Haslemere. Lübeck is a charming town, of a peculiar cold, light coloring of yellow and pale green plaster houses, dominated by great brick churches, whose clear, whitewashed interiors are filled with rich monuments of the past Hanseatic prosperity — sculptured marbles, paintings, carved and gilded wood, elaborate astronomical clocks and great organs, all in a peculiar North German austere exuberance, exactly like the music of Bach and Buxtehude. In the evening I went with the organist (whom I had met at the von Beckeraths') into the Marienkirche, whose high white vaults and dim monuments were illuminated by the cold light of the waxing moon. We mounted the creaking stairs to the organ loft where by the light of a candle stub I kept the bellows full and he played the magnificent "Totentanz" organ, an instrument of unspoiled seventeenth-century richness and clarity of tone.

Friday afternoon I played a magnificent Steingräber harpsichord, the best instrument I have found in Germany. Unfortunately only six exist, and the maker is dead. Later in the afternoon I went out to Bergedorf to visit the son of the editor of the Händelgesellschaft, in the hope of obtaining some of the volumes for which I have long been vainly searching. I found him, a slightly childish, senile old man, in a little cottage surrounded by chickens and his father's magnificent library. He was very nice to me, showed me the library and the plates of the Händelgesellschaft (which he will not give into the hands of a publisher for reprint), indulged in wandering reminiscences, presented me with a glass of wine, a bunch of violets and two dried apples. I finally came away rather late, with two complete volumes of chamber music, and a few stray sheets containing the long sought violin sonatas.

Saturday at an abominably early hour, I left Hamburg for Göttingen, where I spent the afternoon and evening with Saunders, and enjoyed as before the stimulation of his penetrating mental clarity.

Sunday I went on to Eisenach, where I visited the birthplace of Bach, and solved in no way the riddle of the rise of such a genius out of such a "spiessbürgerlich" environment. . . .

Monday I came to Jena, where I had been invited (railway fare to be paid) by the Glaser harpsichord makers. Although I found the instrument in many ways unsatisfactory and not pleasing in tone, I was considerably encouraged by the eagerness of the people to take criticism, and by their anxiousness to furnish me later (apparently free) with an instrument which should meet all my desires (if they are capable of it). I had rather hoped they would offer to send an instrument to Italy, in spite of my dissatisfaction with it, but they seemed to regard Italy as barren ground. However, they had a brilliant idea about the vacant harpsichord teaching position in the Salzburg summer school, and are exerting all their influence to get it for me.

My regret at leaving Germany is considerably lessened by my recent improvement in the language, which I now speak perfectly easily, so that, for example, in Hamburg I felt completely at home. If only I knew Italian as well!

[From Weimar and Jena I proceeded southward, stopping in Bamberg, Nürnberg and Munich. I have transposed to a chronological order of events the following excerpts from a long letter written on the train between Florence and Rome and finished in Rome.]

19 Maggio 1933   On the train from Florence to Rome

So here I am in a third-class compartment with seven Italians (who, I hope, won't ruin this letter by desiring to turn out the light and go to sleep, for I have enough to write to keep me busy until morning). Even now the seven Italians express their admiration at my temerity in attempting to write on the train.

I believe I last wrote from Bamberg. I spent a delightful day there, enjoying the expanding influence of early spring sunshine and the enchanting winding hilly streets and old houses of the refreshingly Catholic town.

. . . an excellent performance of *Don Giovanni* in the Residenztheater, a delicious rococo building of 1754, decorated with mellowed paintings and much old gold.

The next morning I left for Venice. The clouds were low and it rained a little as we came over the German side of the mountains, but as we rolled down into Italy the golden afternoon sun glowed like a benediction on my Nordic soul and I gazed into the glorious blue Italian distances with considerable elation. And I found the Italians so charming.

At Brennero for the customs inspection I was obliged to open my clavichord which glowed like a blue green peacock in the shabby baggage car, and as I demonstrated it with a few chords the bright-eyed Italians took in their breath and murmured "Bella."

At midnight I shivered my way in the steamboat up the black and glittering Grand Canal and recognized with all the joy of a year's nostalgia the ghostly white of the Rialto bridge, and later of the Salute and, as I landed, of the dim white arcades of the Ducal Palace and the shining mosaics and marbles of San Marco.

I have forgotten the chronology of the next weeks except that I had three glorious days of sunshine full of all the wonderful effects of light and color that the city has to offer, followed by three days of rain in which I sopped about with perpetually wet feet vainly trying to see faded paintings in dim church interiors. I saw many paintings which I had not seen before, especially of Carpaccio and Tiepolo, and revisited the Academy, the Ducal Palace and certain churches with renewed delight. Unfortunately, on account of the cloudy weather and bad light I made a completely vain visit to the great Tintorettos in San Rocco and did not even attempt to see those in S. M. dell' Orto. But I was more than ever impressed by certain pictures in the Academy and spent half a day repeatedly returning to five glorious pictures of Tintoretto and Titian in the Ducal Palace. It is so annoying not to be able to have a painting with one like a book of poetry or a score of music, but to be obliged in half an hour to attempt to some degree to fix it in the memory. For this reason I either made crude sketches or returned to certain paintings repeatedly.

I had one glorious late afternoon at S. Giorgio Maggiore, first with one of the most thrilling pictures in the world, the Tintoretto "Martyrdom of SS. Cosmas and Damian," and then with the unbelievable light and color of the lagoons and the islands seen from the tower in the slanting late sun. Such blues, greens and lavenders and pinks, all translucent and seeming to float like a mirage! Then, surrounded, as when I wrote last year, by bargaining gondoliers, I watched the sunset fade behind Santa Maria della Salute. As I neared the Riva degli Schiavoni in my gondola, a most extraordinary thing occurred. It began to darken and as the lights of the anchored ships began to appear, a thick silent mist swept in from the sea with terrifying rapidity and engulfed first San Giorgio, then all the ships, leaving the domes of Sta. Maria floating as gray fantastic shadows in the distance. Presently these disappeared and the water took on a ghostly silver luminosity melting into the dull soft gray of the mist.

And then it rained for three days, with occasional moments of light and real Venice color, with the gray and pink houses and lavender wisteria reflecting themselves through a net of white bridges in the still water. At other times even in the rain the water of the canals was a dense light blue green like the interior of my clavichord. . . .

The evenings I spent walking about the winding streets and up and down the steps of bridges, sitting in the Piazzetta looking out over the water, or on the bridge behind San Marco watching the Venetians and the tourists and the sailors pass, respectively on their way to cafés, hotels and brothels. Often I rather regretted having sent my clavichord direct to Rome, but I had been frightened by the problem of transportation from station to hotel, not having thought of the picturesque if alarming prospect of loading it into a gondola.

(At this point the Italians, with politeness but firmness, put the light out and went to sleep. I am now standing in the corridor.)

It was rather a contrast to come from the gorgeously unmoral and exuberant Venice into the sober and austere Padua, to revisit the Mantegna frescoes in the Eremitani* with heightened appreciation, to stand in wonder before the Donatello (alas, difficult to see this year, because of bad light) and to spend a morning with the Giotto frescoes in the Arena chapel. I also revisited the three early Titians in the Scuola del Santo, having almost forgotten how marvelous they were.

From Padua I took the noon train to Florence, through beautiful mountain landscape with bare terraced hills thinly cloaked with grapevines and pale gray-green olive trees, with blue shadowed mountains in the distance. Finally we came to the long winding way down through the Tuscan hills into Florence. Florence is a sober warm brown gray noble, aristocratic city with weatherbeaten bridges and picturesque houses framing the water of the Arno the color of thick yellowish pea soup.

[I quote the following as an example of the unfavorable first impressions that it is possible to receive from persons who afterwards reveal themselves in quite other aspects, and who become kind and loyal friends. By June 15 I was writing: "In the evening I had dinner and played at the Berensons'. This time the clavichord sounded slightly better upstairs in the library, and I quite liked Mr. and Mrs. Berenson, who were very nice to me. On the whole it was a very delightful evening."]

19 Maggio 1933   On the train from Florence to Rome

Today has been a curious day, first practicing the clavichord and playing certain pieces like a pig, then going out to lunch at Bernard Berenson's villa and playing the clavichord there. My resolution, inspired by "North," "Central," and "Florentine Painters of the Renaissance" and certain disgusting art catalogues, to pull Mr. Berenson's nose on meeting him, had been somewhat weakened by Roger Sessions' admiration, but I must say that today I disliked him

* destroyed by bombing in World War II

111

and the atmosphere of his home heartily. True, he has a marvelous house and garden, superb paintings of Martini, Lorenzetti, Giotto (?) and others, as his fancy leads him to change the attributions (!), and a library almost incredible for its size and contents as well. But the atmosphere is a little too ungenuinely rarefied and he is nevertheless a parvenu, who for all his intellectual ability made himself a great man through the occupation of writing catalogues for American millionaires to the effect that "although we cannot attribute this painting to Giotto, it is just as good" (and I add, "and worth as much"); and like my educators at Harvard, to paraphrase Virginia Woolf "creeps like a maggot in and out of the skulls" of generations of great artists. But perhaps this is because he made me uncomfortable and my clavichord sounded like the devil in his drawing room full of Sassettas and Chinese bronzes. I may like him better next time.

Then I got home and found a telegram informing me of difficulties with the harpsichord in Rome, obliging me to cancel the rest of my Florentine engagements and hasten to Rome. . . . So here I am in a third class compartment, being sped on my way with a glittering Italian smile from the porter to whom I had given too large a tip.

I have so hopelessly much to write about, but I suppose I can give my bewildered historical sense a little encouragement by attempting to begin at the beginning. (If it is any use. As you see, the Appenines are VERY bumpy. One consolation — if I am again led to procrastinate so long, I shall know that you are still only about half way through my last letter! . . . (the Italians have just turned on the light and have invited me back with various allusions to "costanza" and talk of "un secondo Dante") . . .

Rome [in front of the Villa Medici]

It is so nice to be sitting on something stable, even if it is only a cold block of stone against an ilex tree. (The Italians inquired all about my life and works and became very friendly and offered the "caro americano" cookies, oranges and godawful candy.)

Although my first impressions of Rome were rather unfavorable, I now think of it as an enchanting city, like nearly all Italian cities, with its own strongly pronounced individual character. The ruins are not as I had from childhood imagined, gray and sepia-colored, but

112

full of warm weatherbeaten color, overgrown with grass; the houses and churches are built of warm stone, or of an enchanting pink-orange plaster with elemental white stone; and the whole city is scattered with delicious fountains and exuberant baroque churches.

Here I am in the afternoon sun on the Janiculum hill looking across at the grassy slopes and pine and cypress trees of what I (probably wrongly) assume to be the Villa Lante, and at the great dome of San Pietro. Behind me stretches the vast brown and pink expanse of Rome, with hazy blue mountains behind.

6 Giugno 1933
. . . then we went to San Pietro. The vast interior was completely filled with people, the great pilasters hung with red brocade, the crossing kept clear by the pi-colored Swiss guards, and the choir behind the great bronze ciborium ablaze with candles and electric lights. Above us the dome soared to a dizzy height and a few white clouds were visible through the high transept windows. The baroque saints ecstatically twisted and curled and the crowd babbled expectantly. Across the nave sat the bronze Saint Peter in archaic solemnity, clad for the day in white robes and golden tiara which left only the black face visible, looking like a Hottentot on Sunday. Presently trumpets were heard and the people hastily clambered onto benches and pilaster bases, and from far down the nave came great waves of applause. Then gorgeously clad choir boys appeared and cardinals in their purple robes, and finally, borne like an ivory idol in a great high chair, the Pope himself, who lifted his right hand in the gesture of blessing with all the benign regularity of a robot. The applause was tremendous. Mothers held up their children and everyone cried "Viva il Papa!", until the procession disappeared into the choir, and the sounds of the crowd faded into the sentimental music of the service.
As we came out into the vast Piazza, we found the evening sky full of warm clear sunset clouds, which we watched from the Gianicolo fade into silvery gray over the rooftops and the black cypresses.

113

[I then returned to Florence.]

Monday I was invited to lunch and to play the clavichord at Mrs. Loeser's* house, a very luxurious villa, not always in the best of taste, but containing some marvelous works of art, sculpture of Jacopo della Quercia, Rosselino, Bernini, some old harpsichords, an early Dolmetsch clavichord and some fourteen paintings of Cézanne, and many excellent Italian paintings. Mrs. Loeser was enormously pleased with my playing (she is a pianist herself) and invited me to come and stay with her and to play in her house. I have seldom heard my clavichord sound so well as it did in her great hall.

Tuesday I again went out to the Villino for tea and supper. There for the first time I made the acquaintance of Roger's music. I found parts of the Piano Sonata and all of the unfinished Violin Concerto exceedingly beautiful. In the evening as we walked down to the tramway in the hushed starlight, I heard for the first time nightingales singing in the cypresses. . . .

[Once again I returned to Rome.]

After winding up affairs in Rome (and throwing ten centesimi in the Acqua Trevi!) I went out to Tivoli to the Villa d'Este. Any paradise conceivable to the human mind could hardly surpass this garden with its terraces and landscape vistas, its glorious sunshine, few choice flowers, towering cypresses and blue sky, and the rustle and murmur of innumerable fountains, so that the very ground seems to pulsate. I sat in the dappled shadows and watched a high jet of water sparkle in the sun against the sky and dark trees, and breathed in the odor of boxwood and roses, and loved Italy as I never had before.

My Italian is in a far from satisfying state, yet I really have learned a great deal since I came. I shall be very happy when I finally have a command of it. Even now I can carry on conversations of an elementary nature and read the newspapers.

I almost dread the nostalgia I shall feel for this country next winter. I think I shall never be really content until I can come and live here for some time. When I look back at the last weeks, I can

* Olga Loeser, a friend of Berenson

hardly believe the richness of my experiences. And when I think of what lies across the river here in Florence still for me to see! Although there has been hardly a direct musical advantage in coming to Italy, I find more than ever that my experiences in the visual arts act consciously through direct parallels on my musical conceptions, and also that the inspiration passes over in many less tangible ways, in spite of my new-grown distrust of people who mix up the arts or dissipate in too many directions the cultivation of perfection. But I have found not only the works of art so wonderful, but also something in the people and in the atmosphere of the country, a perfectly free, suave and natural function of the feelings and sentiments, a freedom from the cramped mis-discipline of the North. Somehow, without the moral strain and intellectual effort of northern Puritanism one simply sits by a fountain and feels the effortless unintellectual reintegrating influences sinking in with the warmth of the sun and the sound of water and the sight of cypress trees against the blue sky.

Epilogue

THE YEARS WITH RALPH

Frederick Hammond

I

Even in the age of the recording industry, the performing musician is one whose name is "writ in water." Therefore, it may be necessary to inform the casual reader of this book that Ralph Kirkpatrick was the most distinguished harpsichord and clavichord player of his generation, and a scholar who restored Domenico Scarlatti to rank with J.S. Bach and François Couperin as a keyboard composer. Kirkpatrick's influence was felt far beyond the narrow boundaries of the early music world in performance, teaching, scholarship, and instrument design and building.

The publisher of this book has asked me, as Ralph's literary executor, to round out the picture presented by the text, which describes Ralph's family background and his life through his first European trip in 1931–33. (The rest, he used to say, was mostly "concerts played and meals eaten.") This in turn requires a bit of autobiography. I first met Ralph in 1953 at the age of sixteen, when I summoned up the courage to introduce myself after one of his Scarlatti recitals in New York's Town Hall. I had planned to enter the Yale School of Music (then a professional rather than a graduate school), but on the evidence of my high school transcript Ralph strongly advised me to pursue a liberal-arts major in Yale College. He not only communicated this advice to my father, but also arranged for the necessary late admission and financial aid — an act of imaginative generosity that determined the subsequent course of my life. At the end of my first year he wrote in my copy of his *Domenico Scarlatti*: "For Fred Hammond, who promises to be one of the few to understand the implications of Chapter XIV [the chapter on performance], with every fond hope and wish for the realization of that and other promise."

During my undergraduate years at Yale I combined a full academic program with weekly lessons and regular solo recitals, much as Ralph had done during his undergraduate career at Harvard. His twenty-fifth reunion fell in 1956, and his interest in me may have been in part a vicarious reliving of his own college years. Our backgrounds were similar: we both came from literate small-town families with a smattering of music, we both escaped to great universities that proved to be the opening of an immeasurably richer life, we both graduated at twenty and headed for Europe. In some cases the parallels extend even to details: Ralph gave his first paid concert in 1933 in Bernard Berenson's library at the Villa I Tatti, and thirty-two years later I played my first Italian recital in the same room, and to some of the same people.

At the close of these memoirs in 1933 Ralph had formed a personal character and a musical technique but not yet a career. The latter was accomplished slowly and with periods of great financial hardship. In the summer of 1933 he taught at the Mozarteum in Salzburg, where he continued to perfect his command of the clavichord and fortepiano. His activities widened to include ever more prominent appearances in Europe and then in the United States as soloist and continuo player. (Ralph gave me his score of the Bach *St. Matthew Passion*, purchased in Berlin in 1932 and signed by Bruno Walter after performances with the New York Philharmonic in 1943, 1944, and 1945.) With the violinist Alexander Schneider, Ralph formed a duo that performed and recorded the major repertory for violin and harpsichord, the sonatas of Bach, Handel, and Mozart. Their appearances at Dumbarton Oaks brought them into contact with Igor Stravinsky — indeed, Ralph's recording of the Manuel de Falla Concerto for Harpsichord, which had a galvanic effect on many young musicians, preserves a Dumbarton Oaks performance coached by Stravinsky himself.

After teaching briefly at Bennington in 1938, Ralph became a member of the faculty of the Yale School of Music in 1940, a year that also marked the arrival of Paul Hindemith at Yale. This association with a distinguished university provided the necessary comple-

118

ment to Ralph's increasingly active performing career and stimulated eventually his work on the Scarlatti biography. He lived as a Fellow in Jonathan Edwards College, then the epicenter of musical activity in undergraduate Yale, and participated eagerly in the vivacious social and intellectual life of the College and the University. In the early 1950's Ralph built a small house on a headland overlooking Long Island Sound, which gave him increased scope for books, collecting fine prints, cooking and entertaining.

The year in which I met Ralph, 1953, signalled a new stage in his career. The Princeton University Press published his massive biography of Domenico Scarlatti to almost universal acclaim for its profound scholarship, musical insight, and fine writing. Schirmer issued Ralph's model edition of sixty of the Scarlatti sonatas — the first modern *Urtext*. And Ralph performed the sixty in a triptych of recitals in New York and New Haven, broadcast them, and recorded them for Columbia. By directing the full force of his authority as both scholar and performer, Ralph had effected single-handedly the renaissance of a major composer.

The success of the Scarlatti projects and Ralph's growing prominence in Germany and Austria led to a contract with Deutsche Grammophon to record all of the Bach harpsichord works. Most of these had been in his repertory for years. His first recording was the three-part Ricercar from *The Musical Offering*, and a decade before the German project he had recorded parts I, II, and IV of the *Clavieruebung* — the six Partitas, Italian Concerto and French Ouverture, and the Goldberg Variations — for the Hadyn Society. The greatest challenge was the recording of both books of the *Well-Tempered Clavier* on both harpsichord and clavichord. Typically, he attacked the project not only at the keyboard, but also by devoting to the *Well-Tempered Clavier* his tenure as the first Ernst Bloch Lecturer at the University of California, Berkeley. Ralph regarded the two versions of both books as his finest achievement. The harpsichord version has recently been reissued,* and the lectures have been published as *Interpreting Bach's Well-Tempered Clavier: An Interpreter's Discourse of Method.*

* Quarry Communications, P.O. Box 3168, Stony Creek, Connecticut 06405

During these years, which corresponded with my departure from Yale and Ralph's extended absences for recordings and concerts, our friendship was cordial but casual. We met in Rome in 1972, when Ralph played at Santa Cecilia, dined in the company of two Roman princesses, sat long over strawberries and Frascati in the Piazza Farnese, and made a memorable trip in my ancient Fiat to the museum at Palestrina. Ralph announced that this was the first time in months that his eyes had been able to perceive details from a moving car. In 1973 he came to perform at UCLA, playing Sebastian, my large Dowd harpsichord, and we celebrated together on Scarlatti's birthday the twentieth anniversary of the publication of *Domenico Scarlatti*. Ralph was clearly having physical and visual problems, but he managed to read and to approve cautiously my sketch for a life of Girolamo Frescobaldi.

In 1975 I received a letter from Ralph announcing the imminence of open heart surgery and asking me to act as his literary executor if necessary. That operation was a success, but the following year Ralph went completely blind from glaucoma. Although this had been a possibility for years, nevertheless its effect on a man whose career and avocations were so tied to the visual must have been catastrophic. From then on my own life was as closely tied with Ralph's as time and distance permitted, and I never saw any sign of self-pity. Clearly, Ralph was also the son and brother of experimental observers. Wherever possible, the processes of orientation to a now-invisible environment, learning Braille, storing and retrieving information, were treated as matters of abstract scientific interest. In the words of Emerson's essay on Self-Reliance (a formative document for Ralph's character), "To talk of reliance is a poor external way of speaking. Speak rather of that which relies, because it works and is."

I once facetiously compared Ralph to Oedipus at Colonus, a suggestion that he rejected coldly. And yet, like Oedipus, Ralph both suffered and occasionally did terrible things (see page 56 of the text). And, like Oedipus, he was finally rewarded beyond any imagining — not with an assumption to the divine, but by the appearance of Christian Foy, a professional instructor for the blind, who became Ralph's companion and dearest friend. This meant not only that

Ralph could continue to live in his own house, but also that the world he no longer could get out to meet easily could be entertained there, and that he could benefit from every advance in skill and technology for the blind.

In 1977 Ralph began to undertake concert performing again. After a semi-private appearance at Versailles, he made his first public appearance at the Frick Collection in New York. I heard from observers that he had almost fallen from the tiny platform, and that he had started the opening work in the wrong key. His own account was that "the only difficulties were finding the harpsichord, and finding middle C." His second public concert took place at UCLA, again on Sebastian. I was virtually crippled by a back injury, and Ralph was still in the first stages of assimilating his blindness, but nonetheless my memories of his stay evoke delightful evenings – the reading of a risqué poem by W.H. Auden finished (I hope) just as a lady guest arrived for dinner, or the halt and the blind helpless with laughter while trying to deal with a stoppage in the plumbing.

During this visit we concocted a plan for Ralph's return to active touring in Europe. Since I was scheduled to perform there the following summer and thus would have a large instrument available, I would take a quarter's leave of absence in order to function as truck-driver, technician and tuner, and courier. The trip is described in a letter of November 1977:

> RK was supposed to turn up in Rome from Germany on the 24th, so I went north to pick up Sebastian and come down to Rome to meet him. Instead, I encountered him and Chris (the 'mobility instructor') on the Accademia bridge. We spent a few days in Venice (this is Chris' first trip to Europe), then Florence and Rome via Orvieto . . . There have been some difficult moments, as this is RK's first real contact – intensified by seeing it through Chris – with the world of art for which he has had a passion since he first came here in 1932 and which he can no longer see . . . The playing is beautiful: tonight he plays a program for the [American] Academy – Handel, Rameau, Bach, Scarlatti. The tour proper starts on Friday with Santa Cecilia, then two programs in Palermo, followed by Modena, Imola, Pescara, Ancona and Venice, mostly at two-day intervals, which in some cases will mean heavy driving for me . . . tuning and regulating are complicated by the fact that Ralph wants to do it all. . . .

Many of the scenes described by Ralph in these memoirs are inter-cut for me with memories of this first trip. In Palermo he played in an overwhelming Baroque church, a gigantic oval soup-tureen veneered in rose, black, and gold marble, and wondered at the exquisite manners of the young audience. "Imola," I wrote, "which one might have expected to be the end of the world, was delightful, not so much for the town as for the theater and above all the hospitality of the local concert-headers, who entertained us royally and provided a real glimpse of the best kind of provincial, middle-class (neither of these pejoratives) desire for culture and good manners." Pescara, on the other hand, was "a seaside town with no attractions except that of getting the laundry done."

Our trip to Venice was an Odyssey in itself, one that Ralph often made me recount as a party piece. We had lunch in Chioggia and set off for Venice in ever-increasing rain. I parked our truck illegally in the Piazzale Roma and got us and our seven suitcases deposited in a motor-launch. We and the baggage were decanted onto the float of our hotel on the Grand Canal — a process made no easier by the storm, Ralph's solid build, and his habit of traveling wrapped in a black loden cloak. I settled him in his room and went to deal with my harpsichord, which was ferried in an open boat under the pouring rain to the site of the concert, the Palazzo Labia. I returned to the hotel, where my progress across the room was perceptible to Ralph as a series of squishes, and after a restorative drink or two we went down to dinner. The waiters wore hip-boots and announced that dessert would not be served as the ground floor of the hotel was flooding. I settled Ralph for the night, checked my shoes and socks with the concierge, rolled up my trousers, and set out for a walk in the *acqua alta*. The first thing I saw on leaving the hotel was a drowned rat.

The next morning Ralph set to work at the Palazzo, practising in the room decorated by Tiepolo with the story of Anthony and Cleopatra. Although we had solemn promises that all official formalities had been taken care of, Ralph was told that he had to register with the police or risk ending up in jail if he played the concert. Ignoring his refusal and predictable rage, I was sent off with his passport in an official launch to catch the *Questura* before it closed. Despite this and other provocations (especially the ineptitude of the official tuner), the concert was superb and highly successful. Wrapped in cloaks, we wandered back to the hotel through the ghostly loveliness of a Venetian fog, absorbed in the performer's eternal search for some place to eat afterward.

As we followed the movers down the staircase of the palace the next morning, Ralph put his hand on the frescoed wall and asked, "What am I touching?" On reading the account of his arrival in Venice in 1933, "up the black and glittering Grand Canal," I recall his departure down the same Canal on a brilliant December morning nearly a half-century later, the two of us on the housetop of a cargo boat with the harpsichord spread out on the deck below.

We made two German trips. The first started in Echternach in Luxemburg and ended in Munich, where Ralph was to play in the eighteenth-century Schloss Schleissheim. Chris and I visited Dachau, and the three of us heard a lovely performance of *Die Zauberflöte* — surely two potent images of the warring strains in the German character. The following year we stayed in the Hotel Continental in Munich ("sehr untergegangen"), where Ralph had signed the Deutsche Grammophon contract. That year's concert took place in Schloss Dachau, a pleasure palace in a pretty town a few miles from the concentration camp. The temporary stage was a small high platform reached by a steep stairway and initially covered with carpet. (A blunt "Ich spiele nicht auf Teppich" took care of that.) At the end of the program Ralph toiled out for a first encore, then for a second, and announced in German, "What I am about to play is not an encore, but a memorial," and began the heart-rending chromatic minor variation from the Goldbergs. Around me people of my own age sat in tears, but after the performance a young man came up to ask, "Is it permitted to inquire to what was the memorial?" I could only stammer, "I thought that was obvious."

As a compulsive teacher, Ralph was concerned to supply our deficiencies in German art. The routes of both tours were arranged so that we could visit monuments such as Ottobeuron, Würzburg for the Tiepolo frescoes, Vierzehnheiligen, Colmar for the Isenheim altarpiece, Reims (Ralph's first visit in 1932 is described in the memoirs), Strasbourg, Nymphenburg. Despite the pain that such visits must have cost Ralph, he not only accompanied us but also demonstrated anew his extraordinary visual memory, as when at Ottobeuron he recited in order the subjects of the ceiling fresco.

During these years the work on my own book, *Girolamo Frescobaldi*, progressed slowly. Tours were enlivened — if that is the word — by readings from the work in progress, with careful criticism from Ralph. At a dinner party in Paris I asked permission to dedicate the book to him, to which he responded by bursting into tears. When it finally appeared, he and Chris celebrated the occasion for me by an elegant dinner, at which Ralph presented me with the 1745 edition of Gasparini's *L'armonico pratico al cimbalo*, one of the first theoretical works to rank Frescobaldi as a model keyboard composer, and one in whose composition Domenico Scarlatti is thought to have had a hand. Ralph had bought it in Florence in 1933 and inscribed his name proudly on the flyleaf. Fifty years later he had added painfully, "For Fred, this link between Frescobaldi and Scarlatti." I like to think that the "every fond hope and wish for the realization of that and other promise" expressed in 1953 had been justified, at least in part.

II

Ralph Kirkpatrick went to Europe in 1931 for two professional purposes: to complete his musical training, and to recreate the technique of the harpsichord, clavichord, and early piano from every available practical and theoretical source. Today, given the resources of American universities and conservatories, such a decision would seem superfluous. But in 1931 Europe was still the center both of advanced musical training and of the still-nascent early music movement.

The protagonists of Ralph's European program are introduced rather casually into his text. For the completion of his overall musicianship the obvious choice was "Mademoiselle" — Nadia Boulanger (1887–1979), whose training had a formative influence

124

on generations of musicians as diverse as Roger Sessions, Aaron Copland, Elliott Carter, and Ned Rorem. Her implicit philosophy that the progressive fine-tuning of musical perception was the gateway to any higher musical accomplishment was the basis of Ralph's teaching.

In the area of recovering the construction, technique, and performance practice of early keyboard instruments the choices were less clear. At least three contrasting schools of thought existed, and Ralph sampled and − as his letters show − tried to combine all three. The most consipicuous was that of the charismatic Wanda Landowska (1879−1959), established in an Ecole de Musique Ancienne at St. Leu-la-Forêt with a collection of instruments and a throng of admiring disciples. As early as the late nineteenth century Parisian piano-makers had begun to copy eighteenth-century French harpsichords, but under Landowska's influence their product was transformed by a powerful dose of modern piano technology − metal frames, heavy cases, "improved" playing and tuning mechanisms, and the introduction of a sixteen-foot register.

Owing to the Bach revival, under way since the 1820's, Germany occupied a special position in the rediscovery of early music. Ralph seems to have found his German mentors the least inspiring of his teachers. In compensation, he experienced the music of Bach as a living tradition, although one revered even more as Religion than as Art. German harpsichord-builders had evolved an "ideal" instrument based on a harpsichord allegedly once the property of J.S. Bach. This was characterized by the inclusion of a sixteen-foot register on the lower manual and the relegation of the four-foot to the upper keyboard. Both have since been shown to be inauthentic, but Ralph adopted the specifications of this instrument for the suggested registrations in his 1938 edition of the Goldberg Variations. Even the late Deutsche Grammophon recordings display his weakness for the reliability and availability of German harpsichords. The two versions of both books of the *Well-Tempered Clavier*, however, were recorded on more authentic and musically satisfying instruments.

Ralph's most fruitful European experience was that of the "English" school of early music as embodied in the Swiss-French Dolmetsch family. In their house at Haslemere in Surrey they made recorders, viols, harpsichords and clavichords, and presented regular concerts of early music. Arnold Dolmetsch (1858–1940) had been given his own atelier in two piano factories, the Chickering in Boston and the Gaveau in Paris, and by common consent the instruments that he produced there and in his earlier years at Haslemere rank among the finest before the Boston revival of harpsichord building in the 1950's. Dolmetsch remained essentially faithful to the classic traditions of harpsichord construction — wooden frames, closed bottoms, light cases, appropriate string tension, historical mechanisms.

Ralph had already come to know Dolmetsch's instruments during his years at Harvard. Dolmetsch built him a clavichord in 1931, still a lovely and wonderfully responsive instrument, and Ralph later acquired two Dolmetsch/Chickering harpsichords, formerly the property of Violet Gordon Woodhouse and Ferruccio Busoni. (All three instruments are now in the Yale Collection of Musical Instruments.)

The recovery of harpsichord and clavichord technique described in Ralph's letters may also seem an unnecessary labor in an age when the student, with the investment of a few dollars, can practice his finger-exercises according to sixteenth-century Spanish, seventeenth-century Italian, or eighteenth-century French fingerings at will. In 1931, however, the historical bases for these various techniques were still little-known and were imparted through the sometimes idiosyncratic understandings of individual teachers.

Ralph sought a perfection of his general keyboard technique as well as a command of historical approaches. His own innate advantages were unusual. He had a huge hand, capable of spanning a twelfth and of trilling slowly in octaves. Unlike many large hands, however, the fingers had extraordinary articulation and tapered at the ends. From Landowska, Ralph received mostly exercises for strength and dexterity. The harpsichord-oriented French school was not interested in the subtleties of clavichord touch — when Ralph began to perform publicly on the clavichord, Landowska's comment was, "What a pity he can't afford a harpsichord." The English school opened to Ralph the richness of possibilities within the limited dynamic range of clavichord sound, and throughout his career he differentiated completely the touch and musical characteristic of the two instruments.

In Germany Ralph had access to early pianos, and he was a generally unacknowledged forerunner in the current vogue of the fortepiano. He commissioned an instrument from John Challis, not a copy but an "historical interpretation," on which he performed Haydn and Mozart and recorded a number of works: the Mozart concerto K. 453; a program of solo Mozart works; and, with Jennie Tourel, the Haydn cantata *Arianna abbandonata* and a group of Haydn English songs. The slow movement of the concerto − one of the loveliest Mozart recordings in existence − was the occasion of the first splice in Ralph's recording career.

Like many harpsichordists of his generation, Ralph had a wistful attraction to the modern piano. Having learned everything that he needed from eighteenth-century pianos, he was content to perform that repertory on good modern instruments. For the delectation of his friends he spent his summers putting together programs of Beethoven, Schubert, Schumann, Chopin and Liszt. Occasionally he ventured even farther afield, as when he played the piano part in the premiere of Stravinsky's charming Septet. (He also recorded the harpsichord part in the original recording of *The Rake's Progress*, except for a few measures contributed by the late Paul Jacobs.) In his later years Ralph increasingly repudiated in the early music movement what he felt to be musical ineptitude masked by phoney antiquarianism ("the next thing you know they'll be doing *Winterreise* with a counter-tenor and a rattletrap piano"). By the same token, his admiration increased for the musicianship of performers such as Pinchas Zuckerman and Alfred Brendel. We encountered the latter at the Residenz in Würzburg, but the long luncheon that he and Ralph promised each other never materialized.

In this memoir I may seem to have emphasized too much the anecdotal and the purely personal. Certainly, Ralph was not only one of the greatest musicians of his time but a man of formidable intellect as well − a connoisseur of the visual arts, a noted print-collector, a reader who knew the literatures of France, Germany, Italy and Spain in their original languages and ranged from *Paradise Lost* to *Finnegans Wake* in English. Nonetheless, as the many accounts of the last years of Bernard Berenson and Igor Stravinsky show, with age the components of the great man tend to separate themselves. The achievements of the external career take on a life of their own; the increasingly fragile human being acquires an individual importance and a separate poignance. And his departure leaves a void that even the legacy of a great career can never entirely fill.

Los Angeles
December 1984

128

1. *Edwin and Florence Kirkpatrick with their children Clifford, Marian, and Alice, ca. 1903. Courtesy Laird Kirkpatrick.*

2. *Marian Kirkpatrick, ca. 1916.*

3. *Ralph Kirkpatrick, May 1931. Photo by Richard S. Shuman.*

4. RK, Vienna, September 1933.

5. RK, Malcolm Holmes, Alberto Moravia, Erich Hawkins. Salzburg, 1933. Photo by G. Alberti.

6. *RK, Attersee, 1934. Photo by G. Alberti.*

7. *RK, Salzburg, 1934.*

8. RK, Salzburg, 1934. Photo by G. Alberti.

9. RK, New York, 1935. Photo by Silvia Saunders.

10. *RK with his stepmother, Annis Kinsman Kirkpatrick, after a concert in Williamsburg, Virginia.*

11. RK at his home at Old Quarry in Guilford, Connecticut, 1977.